THEATRE MOVEMENT

THEATRE MOVEMENT

THE ACTOR AND HIS SPACE

NANCY KING

FOREWORD BROOKS McNAMARA

Drama Book Specialists (Publishers)
New York

All rights reserved under the International and
Pan-American Copyright Conventions.
For information address:
Drama Book Specialists (Publishers),
150 West 52nd Street, New York, New York 10019.

ISBN 0-910482-28-4
Library of Congress Catalog Card Number: 73-166533

Printed in the United States of America

10 9 8 7 6

ACKNOWLEDGMENTS

No one creates in a vacuum. There are many people who have helped to make this book a reality, and to thank them all, individually, would be impossible. However, the following people made such a direct contribution to this project that I would be remiss if I did not mention them.

I would like to thank Thomas N. Bethell for encouraging my ideas; Brooks McNamara for insisting that I write this book; Martha Hully for helping to make the first draft a reality; and the members of my class in Movement and Non-verbal Communication for trying out and criticising my ideas.

I wish to thank the Instructional Resources Center at the University of Delaware for providing space and lighting equipment; and the following students whose work is shown in the photographs: Karen K. Carter, James B. Davidson, Scott Green, Allison Mills, Jeffrey L. Prather, Grace E. Ressler, Stephen K. Swift, W. David Watson, Larry Washington, Thomas Willey, Theodore Wilson, Rebecca Wittmeyer, and Emitt Woodey.

I must thank Dorothy Sherman for reading and criticising my manuscript. Without her help, producing the final draft would have been much more difficult.

Finally, I would like to thank my husband, Finn Hannover, for his support, and my son, Lance R. King, for his ability to understand how important writing this book was to me, thereby learning to make do under some very trying circumstances.

FOREWORD

Brooks McNamara

In the last few years a great change has taken place in our view of theatre. The assumption of the realistic theatre that the stage should show the world in its typical form no longer seems especially vital today; the experiments of Appia, Craig, Meyerhold, Artaud, Piscator, and Brecht have made it increasingly clear that radical approaches to performance exist as essential alternatives to realism. Recently a powerful sense of "retheatricalization" of performance has come out of the work of the Living Theatre, the Polish Laboratory Theatre, the Bread and Puppet Theatre, the Open Theatre, the Performance Group, and the Theatre of the Ridiculous. The very definition of theatre has been challenged by Happenings and Activities and by the work of such dance innovators as Martha Graham, Alwin Nikolais, and Ann Halprin. The proscenium stage has given way to the arena, the thrust stage, environmental theatres, and performances in "found" spaces; the traditional role the playwright has been questioned by those interested in the creative possibilities of communal theatre projects; and new and radical roles have been assigned to the theatre audience.

The actor has often emerged from contact with this new theatre with a drastically altered vision of himself as performer and of his function in performance. The complex demands being made on his mind, body, and voice have made him call into question many traditional aspects of actor training that no longer seem so central to the process of acting. Time-honored views about movement training for actors are being tested in workshops and seminars. There is an increasing interest in the creative possibilities offered by the study of circus techniques, bio-mechanics, T'ai Chi Ch'uan, and the work of Jaques-Dalcroze, Alexander and Delsarte. It has become plain that actors can no longer merely be taught to move in ways that appear to be logical and motivated in terms of specific characters. Nor can they be presented with problems in movement solely through another discipline such as dance, fencing or mime, or given a limited and specific framework as in the study of period movement and gesture.

It is the search for basic movement techniques that has prompted Nancy King to write THEATRE MOVEMENT: THE ACTOR AND HIS SPACE. For her, the teaching of movement must focus on fundamental exercises which allow the actor to free himself for the creation of character, experimenting and exploring his relationship to the space around him without the additional burden of relating to a play. Because of its dual emphasis on a careful program of exercises and the creative application of those exercises, THEATRE MOVE-MENT is uniquely fitted to the actor faced with the demands of the tradional stage and the complexities and opportunities presented by the new theatre.

New York
1971

CONTENTS

ILLUSTRATIONS

PHOTOGRAPHS BY TOM SHERMAN

THEATRE MOVEMENT

INTRODUCTION

Movement is man's most fundamental means of communication. We move before we talk. We see before we hear. Our impressions of what we see remain with us long after words are forgotten. For this reason, the actor must learn to use his body to reinforce the words he speaks. THEATRE MOVEMENT: THE ACTOR AND HIS SPACE explores imaginative means that can be used to help the actor communicate more effectively. When the actor is able to "physicalize" his own feelings, he can then go on to the more difficult process of creating a specific character who reacts in a specific manner. Freedom comes from training which enables the actor to choose his responses without inner conflict or inhibition.

The activities in this book are basic to good acting. They will enable the actor to work effectively in terms of physical conditioning, energy, and non-verbal communication. He should then be able to bring his full capabilities to rehearsal and performance. Because the process of maintaining peak condition, both physical and mental, never ends, this book can also act as a source of stimulation for more experienced actors.

There are many books and manuals about acting already available. Why should another be necessary? It has been my experience that actors are taught specific acting techniques with no fundamental preparation. Before one can react as a particular character one must be free to react. This freedom comes as the result of training which prepares the actor to be physically flexible and adept, emotionally free to project his feelings, and intellectually confident that his body is ready to work. He must also know how his body works, what it can do, and what it can be trained to do, in order to apply this knowledge without conscious effort.

Most books on acting have sections on movement. Their discussions of movement, however, center on blocking patterns, gesture, and pantomime. Authors readily admit that actors need training in movement, and suggest that the place for this is in a dance studio or a fencing class. Dance, fencing or sport is not, however, the equivalent of movement for actors. The aims, problems, and methods are totally different. Movement training has as its goal the "physicalization" of a particular character in action. A class in movement should enable the student to explore ideas freely without, however, the problem of relating to a play. Only when one knows the vocabulary of the body is one free to choose the right movement for a specific role and situation. This does not mean that there is one fixed way to "physicalize" ideas. Rather, one must discover various ways to support, emphasize (or even deny) the spoken word with movement. The actor needs a clear, concise, effective program of activities that will help him learn to use movement in the fundamental areas of physical conditioning and non-verbal communication. This book attempts to create such a program.

CHAPTER ONE

FUNDAMENTAL OF PHYSICAL CONDITIONING
AND NONVERBAL COMMUNICATION

Movement training has always been a part of the actor's learning experience. From training in movement, the actor expects to improve his basic conditioning (endurance, flexibility, strength, balance, and coordination). He expects to learn about gesture, the physical manifestation of emotion, and to become more poised and relaxed on the stage. Traditionally he could study gymnastics, fencing, ballet, pantomine, and, more recently, modern dance. Although these subjects are valuable to some degree, they do not teach the actor what he must know about movement for his specific needs. Each subject is a complete discipline in itself, requiring the technique he is studying. For example: a forward roll is an important safety skill but it does not help the actor to become less inhibited emotionally. Fencing improves coordination but it does not teach an actor to touch a fellow actor without shyness. Ballet is extremely theatrical, involving the total body in training, but studying its rigid patterns cannot help him to become aware of tension levels (how much energy is being expended). Pantomime will help the student learn to create illusion but it cannot teach him to expand his vocal ability. (Although we are dealing with non-verbal communication this does not imply silent communication.) Modern dance, perhaps the freest of the dance forms, still involves the learning of movement patterns not totally relevant to the actor.

What the actor needs is a program in movement designed solely for him. All of the techniques, patterns, and ideas should be completely designed to fulfill the needs of acting students. This new kind of training should include two basic areas of study: physical conditioning and non-verbal communication. Each facet of the program has a dual focus; the immediate problem and its relationship to the larger purpose: good acting.

Physical Conditioning

Just as a musician needs to practice scales regularly, so an actor must work to keep his body in good physical condition. Physical training has a tradition in the theatre: the Kabuki theatre of Japan and the Kathakali of India are based on the physicalization of ideas and feelings. Directors, from the Duke of Saxe-Meningen through Meyerhold and Grotowski, have continually emphasized the importance of physical conditioning for the actor.

When the student begins to work on the physical exercises, he must always do so with the total body in mind. He must remember that he is strengthening his body to enable him to go beyond his present capabilities. Laurence Olivier has said in an interview with Kenneth Tynan:

> I keep myself very fit now, I have to. I go to a gym twice or three times a week, not merely to look tremendously muscular, but I have to keep fit for my job. I love it. But it's no use pretending it doesn't involve a certain amount of overwork, because it does. I've seen a lot of contemporaries get a bit under the weather with such work and I'm determined not to. Some idiotic, childish reasoning tells me that a strong body means a strong heart and I daresay it will look after me.
>
> (Kenneth Tynan, "The Actor: Tynan Interviews Olivier,")
> Tulane Drama Review, T34 (Winter 1966),p.79

Tynan then asked Olivier what kind of actor he was looking for when he formed the National Theatre Company:

> Very good ones, very good ones. Versatile

ones: people who had their heart in the right place; unlazy ones, deeply enthusiastic, gifted with all sorts of attributes. I must say that the nature of the work, as I said before, does demand physical—not perfection, but physical prowess. It does demand great strength, much more than people think. It demands physical tone. When you get an actor who is gifted with immense strength, his coordination is so much better than a weedy type of actor. We've got an actor, Colin Blakely; he played Philoctetes in a Greek tragedy which didn't succeed very well. But to see this man put one foot up on a rostrum above him, and get up like a lion in the most wonderful gesture of his body, that's the sort of thing we ought to be able to do, to be very physically adept.

(Kenneth Tynan, "The Actor" Tynan Interviews Olivier,")
Tulane Drama Review, T 34 (Winter 1966),p.79)

Non-verbal Communication:

The second area of study is non-verbal communication: the the expression of feelings, attitudes, and emotions through movement. Non-verbal communication includes the study of contact, the use of voice in other than speech, concentration, and relationships. Some acting schools use sensitivity training, such as encounter and T groups. Although this training may be useful, it is not specifically useful to the actor. In any case, sensitivity training is not a substitute for the activities in non-verbal communication in this book. If the actor looks to his training for psychological or therapeutic help, he is better advised to seek professional counsel. Most acting teachers, although well-intentioned, are simply not adequately trained to help their students and to deal with all the ramifications of this kind of experience. One cannot bring people to new experiences and then leave them in the middle of it.

Even when the director tells actors exactly what to do, they are often at a loss to convey what they feel without embarrassment or self-conciousness. It is not very difficult to understand why. The United States, especially, has many unspoken taboos against people touching one another. Men should not kiss men. Women should not hug other women. Actors need to overcome preconceived or culturally imposed ideas involving touching in order to perform with ease anything the script and director require of them. At the same time, it is important to remember that physical sense awareness is not an end in itself. We are concerned only with giving actors the opportunity to explore physical contact so that they are free to use it.

A second area of difficulty concerns the use of the voice. Young actors generally have had little experience with vocal experimentation. They need to have the opportunity to screech, yell, growl, groan, and laugh without being restricted by the specifics of situation or character. This is especially important since some new plays use sound as communication. Many modern plays require a total exploration of self, including non-verbal sounds. For the purpose of our work, the use of speech and sound will come out of emotion related to physical movement. Therefore, no specific exercises on voice alone will be included in the work on non-verbal communication.

The successful use of non-verbal communication depends mainly on the third area of study, the actor's ability to concentrate. This concentration involves the actor's ability to focus on himself, on his partner, and on the group. The ability to divide one's concentration furthers the development of sensitivity which is essential to good ensemble work.

The fourth area of non-verbal communication deals with on-stage relationships. An actor must have a sense of rapport with everyone who shares the stage with him. Through this rapport he becomes sensitive to what everyone else is doing on stage at all times. The director uses this sensitivity to communicate his interpretation of the script. If, for example, an actor screams and is ignored, one atmosphere is created. An entirely different atmosphere is created if the actors on stage pay attention to the screams.

Overlapping the studies of physical conditioning and non-verbal communication is the use of energy. Although a student cannot study energy by itself, he needs to know what it is, how to use it, and how it can be replenished.

Energy:

Energy is a positive force and an active process. For the actor it does not necessarily mean physical activity, but can mean emotional energy. Energy is the force which propels the actor's action and motivation; he must learn to make his energy work for him. Being on stage automatically requires the constant use of energy in varying streams. First, the actor must become sensitive to his personal energy level. From experience one knows that on some mornings it requires great effort just to get out of bed. On such days, the personal energy level is very low. After the student has learned to identify his personal energy level, he must consider the energy level required by the character he is creating. Following this, he is then prepared to learn to regulate the difference between his personal energy level and that of the character. In movement classes students must be taught to produce the appropriate energy on demand.

An actor is always expending energy. When the role requires the character to be physically still, the actor must remain active. While sitting still, the actor should always be involved in listening or thinking. This kind of energy is called emotional energy and is used to create the motivation for his physical condition. For example; there might be a scene where a blind man stands with a cup held ready to receive coins from passers-by. He has no lines and cannot react so actively that he takes away the focus from other actors. He cannot just stand there like a statue however. The actor must ask himself, "What is it like to be dependent on the charity of others? Why is the blind man in the scene? What is his relationship to the others on stage? What are the

9

blind man's specific objectives?'' There are other questions an actor could ask. The point is that once he starts exploring these questions, he will see how much energy he needs to accomplish his non-verbal objectives.

Energy is manifested in two different ways; tension and relaxation.

paralysis caused by fear — tension   relaxation — ease and well-being (energy)

As the diagram shows, tension and relaxation are not two separate states but two parts of a continuum. Tension is the state of intense muscular activity: it implies stress, strain, and tightness. Tension is evoked by many strong emotions, such as fear, anger, and hate. Relaxation is the state of muscular ease: it implies freedom and lack of strain. It is important for the actor to learn to identify the degree of tension necessary for the emotional condition of the character he is portraying. He must also learn to recognize when he is using excessive tension to accomplish his purpose. This enables the actor to understand how to work at a high tension level without losing control. Acting angry on stage differs from being angry on stage because one is personally upset. In terms of physical movement, an actor running on stage, seemingly out of control, knows he must be able to stop abruptly offstage. Thus he must plan how much energy he needs to use and how to taper it off effectively.

The distinction between the actor's energy level and that of the character applies equally to tension and relaxation control. One of the first steps in achieving personal relaxation is to know thoroughly the mechanics of one's role, such as entrances, blocking and cues. The second step is to learn to effect tension in a part of the body while leaving the rest of the body relaxed. When the actor is personally relaxed (enough sleep, proper diet), he can create a greater degree of character tension, using it for longer periods of time, without fatigue. When the student has explored the methods of improving his physical condition, and has understood the concepts involved in non-verbal communication, he is ready for more advanced work in creating the character.

CHAPTER TWO

PREPARING TO WORK

To achieve maximum benefit from the physical exercises in this book the actor must know how to use his kinesthetic sense and must understand the importance of maintaining good body alignment. Once the student knows how to use his kinesthetic sense and can practice good body alignment, he is ready to warm up and begin the physical exercises.

Kinesthetic Sense:

The word kinesthetic comes from the Greek kinein, to move and aisthesia, perception. The kinesthetic sense is the sense that tells you what your body is doing in space through the sensation or perception of movement in the muscles, tendons, and joints. If you close your eyes and put your arm out in front of you, you know it is not behind you because your kinesthetic sense tells you so. This is a very obvious example, but it has direct application for the actor. Dancers are trained to remember movement kinesthetically. They learn their steps by remembering the feel of them. Actors also have movement patterns to learn. They will remember them more easily if they commit them to their movement sense memory, kinesthetically rather than intellectually. This enables them to concentrate on the whole rather than the part.

When an actor becomes aware of all the things his kinesthetic sense tells him, his awareness of himself is greatly increased. He will know when he is using too little tension or when one part of his body is too tense. He will know if his posture is projecting what he wants it to. For example, is he standing very triumphantly, crouching with suspense, or leaning against a gate with great nonchalance? Often the director will tell the actors to improvise some blocking. Many an actor scratches his head in puzzlement when the director says, "That's good, keep it." "Keep what?" the actor thinks. If he has had movement training, he will remember what his movement felt like, and be able to recreate its essence. Sometimes an actor will be involved in a scene whose emotion is somewhat alien to him personally. It will often help him if he begins by learning how his body works while experiencing this emotion. How is his breathing affected? Where is the center of the tension in the body? Does the emotion make him feel open and expansive, or tight and closed off? If he can answer questions like these he will be able to recreate the emotion at will. This is why the actor must know how emotions effect him physically. Too few actors are aware of their movement sense memory or kinesthetic sense.

As soon as the actor starts working on scenes he needs to use his kinesthetic sense in another way. When more than one person is on stage the space between them says something. If they are close to each other they may be very involved. If they are far apart, they may hate each other or not know each other. In a crowd listening to a speaker, the distance between them and the speaker also tells something. If the crowd is far, not separated by a visible barrier, they may feel awe. If their attention is not focused and their group posture is casual, perhaps they are bored. If they are tense as a group and seem to inch forward slowly, perhaps the speaker is in danger. The beginning actor needs to learn awareness of the spaces around him so that they reinforce the action. This dual focus on himself and his fellow actors must be developed from the first rehearsal. The place to learn this focus is in movement class. The actor can also learn a great deal about focus and how situations affect space by observing this in his own life.

Body Alignment:

Improved body alignment or posture is one of the most important contributions of movement training. Body alignment means the proper balancing of the body. When the alignment is correct, an imaginary line running through the vertical of the body will bisect it. The actor checks his body alignment by looking at himself in a full-length mirror. If he sees that he slouches, this is what he will do on stage. He must learn how to correct his alignment without a mirror so that he can make the necessary adjustments on stage using his kinesthetic sense. Bad posture on the stage can ruin the actor's whole performance. A rather extreme example of this happened to a student playing the title role in the morality play EVERYMAN. At the end of the play, Man makes his peace with God and emerges triumphantly. The student playing Everyman had a terrible forward slouch, and when he came forth at the end of the play full of hope and strength he looked like a candidate for a crucifixion. He was leaning into himself, his stomach protruded and, his whole being shouted defeat. His fine diction, vocal range, and good blocking all went for nothing. His body action denied his words.

While doing the physical exercises one must practice good alignment consciously until it becomes habit. The student should first learn the preparatory position which is introduced as the first physical excercise after the section on warmups. If you have been standing improperly for a long time, it will take hard work and concentration to change your natural stance. Do not expect it to happen overnight or even in a few weeks. Improvement will depend on your consistent effort.

Warmups:

After you have prepared yourself to work by starting with the preparatory position, you are ready to warm up. Warmups are exercises used in the beginning of each working period to stimulate the body by increasing the flow of blood to the organs and muscles. Warmups aid in relaxing tense muscles, encourage flexibility, and help prepare the body for more strenuous activity. They also help to focus one's attention on the class or rehearsal, allowing previous events to recede. The warmup exercises should be done without strain or exertion and with a sense of exploration and ease. It is especially important to warm up slowly and carefully if the body is cold or sore from previous workouts.

Sore Muscles:

Sore muscles should be expected. The soreness occurs in muscle fibers that have not been used vigorously for some time. Pain is caused by an accumulation of waste products in the muscle tissue. These waste products can be most effectively reduced by continuing with the exercises daily. The exercise increases the blood supply to the muscles and helps to eliminate the waste products of the previous exercise period. If the muscles are very sore, care should be taken to work gently. Most soreness will disappear entirely after a few days as the body adapts to the new stress. If you should discontinue daily exercise for a few weeks, however, you can expect soreness when you resume. The body cannot store up flexibility, strength, and endurance. This is why dancers, gymnasts, pianists, and others exercise daily to maintain good physical condition.

Preparation:

When you begin to work with the physical exercises, make sure you are starting in the proper position, in good alignment. Read the exercise and do it several times concentrating on what you want to achieve. Stop and read the suggestions after you have tried the exercise. Repeat the exercise and check yourself in a mirror or let a friend watch you. Repeat the exercises again with the suggestions in mind without the mirror and work until you feel ready to stop. When you cannot concentrate on what you are doing, or you begin to work half-heartedly, it is time to stop. It is a good idea to shake out your legs and arms after each exercise or to relax by bending over at the waist with knees bent. Bob up and down gently a few times, then come to a standing position slowly. You will be able to think of other relaxing movements to use between exercises which will help post-pone fatigue. Keep your breathing as even and steady as you can. This will help prevent gasping for breath in the more strenuous exercises. If you have trouble remembering to breathe, try humming or talking to yourself. This has the effect of forcing you to breathe steadily. It also decreases neck strain.

The physical exercises are arranged progressively from easiest to most difficult. Never go on to a harder exercise until you feel you understand and are able to do what is required in the easier exercises. Work slowly and carefully to be sure that you are working correctly. Focus primarily on the mechanics of how you are achieving your desired end result rather than on your eventual goal. For example, if you would like to be able to touch your nose to your knees while sitting with your legs extended you may be tempted to strain and get your head down regardless of the fact that your body is not ready to do this. You may forget to keep your knees extended and to tighten your thighs. You may eventually get your nose to your knees but your way of working is all wrong, and what is worse, your body is not getting the full benefit of the exercise. Do at least one exercise in each section to ensure a complete workout. Wear clothes that permit you to work freely. Try to work in an atmosphere free from distrac-tion and obstacles. How many times you repeat an exercise depends on your physical condition and on the amount of time you have to work. If you are very tired, do not continue. You will not work correctly if you are overtired and there is chance of injury.

The physical exercises are designed first to increase co-ordination, flexibility, balance, strength and endurance. The second purpose is the improvement of kinesthetic awareness so that you begin to know what your body is doing in space at all times. Physical exercise is not an end in itself. One can never exercise a few times and then forget about it. Therefore you must approach the exercises with the idea that they can always be challenging and stimulating. One can always stretch further or jump higher. It may seem that there are too many physical exercises in this book which is concerned with the training of an actor. They are included because as one's body strength changes, one's needs change. An actress trying to get back in shape after pregnancy faces different problems from those of an actor trying to get his legs in shape after a ski injury, or perhaps after he has stopped working for a while. The exercises in this book are non-stylized, based on sound physiological principles and have nothing to do with current theatrical fads. They correspond to the scales a musician practices before he starts working on a particular piece of music.

There is a different format for the physical exercises than for those exercises in the other chapters. This is because the physical exercises must be done exactly as written, in the order suggested. Position is very important and the purpose is defined by section. In the exercises using space and non-verbal communication, position is only suggested. The purpose of each exercise needs to be explained and there is no harm in changing the order.

PHYSICAL EXERCISES—PREPARATORY POSITION

Head

The head should face forward with no strain in the neck.

Shoulders

The shoulders should be down and relaxed. To check this, hunch them up and then let them fall into place. Try this several times.

Arms

The arms should be at your sides with the fingers in an easy (relaxed) position, palms facing inward.

Fingers

In order to check for finger tension rub the middle and ring fingers against each other. This will prevent the accumulation of tension while you are working. Check the fingers often while you are doing any kind of movement activity, especially the new or the difficult.

Stomach

Ease up to create space in the torso between the pelvis and the rib cage. Have a sense of lift in the body. Breathe freely and evenly.

Buttocks and Lower Back

The buttocks should be released. Be careful not to tighten them as this will result in the thighs being pushed forward. Check this in a mirror each time until you can feel when you are working with ease. Lengthen the lower back so the base of the spine can drop.

Legs

The knees should be straight but not locked. The weight is evenly distributed. The feet are on a slight diagonal and a bit apart. Make sure your toes are not clenched.

Practice this position with your side to the mirror, then practice it facing front. Work until you are satisfied that you are correctly aligned. Now close your eyes and see if you can align yourself properly without help from the mirror. Open your eyes and check your position. Try walking, keeping the body in the preparatory position. The important thing to feel is a sense of alertness, balance, and ease within yourself. When potters center they balance the clay on the wheel in order to shape it. The actor must center his body through the preparatory position; it enables him to begin working correctly, with good support from his body. The same principles hold true when sitting, running, or jumping. Work to feel a sense of center, of balance.

WARMUP EXERCISES

There are several basic and common ways of moving which are not dependent on a particular technique. The major ones are stretching, swinging, bouncing, striking, shaking, and collapsing. Considering that these movements can be done quickly or slowly, crouching or on tiptoe, tensely or relaxed, forward, sideways, or backward, one begins to get an idea of the variety of an untrained person's movement. The warm-ups included in this book not only tone the body, but also stimulate creative movement, help establish good group rapport and facilitate proper working conditions for class, rehearsal, and performance.

When you warm up, pay attention to what you find you cannot do well. For example: Are you limited in what you do with your hands, head, and feet in a sitting position? This means that your stomach muscles are weak. Do you wobble when one foot is in the air while standing? You need to strengthen your legs, your torso, and your focus. Use of the warmups regularly, each time you work, will enable you to do more imaginative and complex movements because of increased body control and knowledge.

WARMUP EXERCISES

Stretching

Start out by stretching or extending your whole body in every direction, using your arms, head, legs, fingers, and toes. Move around the room; do not confine yourself to one small area. What is the look of a stretch? What kind of energy do you need to stretch while covering distance? Can you stretch and be relaxed at the same time? In class, if you come into contact with someone who is stretching, try stretching to them without relaxing your energy. What kinds of stretch are possible when you work with a partner or two? How can you stretch when you do not use your arms. What kinds of feelings (if any) do you get when you stretch? What does your body need to do to maintain the stretch while you change levels from high to low, or from up to down? Does stretching make you yawn at first? If it does, it is because the body is calling for an increased supply of oxygen to meet the needs of an active body. The yawn is the way the body responds to this need. Can you stretch with one foot off the floor? What kinds of adjustment in your torso and legs must you make to keep the quality of the stretch and still keep your balance?

WARMUP EXERCISES

Swinging

A swing is a loose, easy relaxed movement that starts with energy, continues because of the momentum of the body, and ends with energy. A swing must have a free flowing ease about it which corresponds to the breathing cycle of inhalation (energy) and exhalation (relaxation of muscles). Try swinging various parts of your body separately: head, shoulders, arms, wrists, waist (upper body), and legs. Can you swing using your whole body? Does your head move with your body, separately, or not at all? If your head does not move with the rest of your body, it is probably because there is strain in the neck. Girls with long hair can enjoy feeling the freedom of the head-swing. Can you make your swing move you around the room? See if you can let the force of your swing swirl you around. If you are fully relaxed while you are swinging, the rhythm of your swing will be different from that of others. Pay attention to your own rhythm. Is it full and expansive or is it tight and cramped? Use extremes of range. Start small and low. Swing to full extension, then reverse the order.

WARMUP EXERCISES

Bouncing

Bounces can be jumps or gentle bobbing, up and down movements done by any part of the body. Bounces must be done
without great exertion and without great range of movement.
Special attention should be paid to correct use of the feet.
One should land, from a jump using first the toe (only for an
instant), then the ball of the foot (metatarsal), the heel, and
finally the bending of the knee. It is absolutely imperative
to follow this sequence, especially if you are working on
concrete or other non-resilient floors. Try bouncing in place,
then moving around the room. The quality of the bounce
should not change when moving forward or backward. Keep
the flow of energy free and easy. Try bobbing the head or
the shoulders. See whether you can bounce from a kneeling
position, sitting on the floor or lying down. If the body does
not "flop" while you bounce, then you know you are tense
and should work to relax your muscles to produce easy,
gentle movements. See what happens when you bounce
another person as if his head were a ball. Bounce with different people in the class, adjusting your rhythm to their
rhythms.

WARMUP EXERCISES

Striking

Striking movements use any part of the body and are short, sharp, clearly defined actions that are the opposite of stretching, languid movements. Although striking motions required organization of the body and a fair amount of tension, they are included in the warmup section because they are part of the basic vocabulary of movement. Another reason for their inclusion is to give the actor a chance to see that he must be personally relaxed in order to effect tension. Striking is often a difficult kind of movement for beginners because it requires a definite commitment; you are either doing the movement or you are not. There is no half way. Try doing this percussive movement in various positions and on various levels. What happens to the quality of the movement when you move across the floor? If you keep your breathing steady, you will find you are less likely to become tense. Remember to keep the movements short, sharp, and crisp. How does working with another person affect you? Does doing this kind of movement in a large group affect the way you feel?

WARMUP EXERCISES

Shaking

Shaking, or vibratory movements, are the hardest to do because they require the greatest muscle control. Shaking movements resemble shivering because they are tiny, quick, and constant. Try shaking in various positions, starting with isolated movements of the arm, leg, or face. If the movements are not extremely rapid, you know you are not vibrating or shaking. You are probably striking. The difference between striking and shaking is the range of motion. When you learn to shake properly you will find it can be very useful in getting rid of fatigue that accumulates in parts of the body that have been worked very hard. For example: if you have been standing on your feet for a long time they will probably feel tired. Lie down on your back, put your legs in the air and shake out your ankles as hard as you can. Stop, then repeat. Do not let your legs drop to the floor when you have finished shaking them out. Bend your knees and place the soles of the feet on the floor. If you have really shaken your ankles, you will feel much less tired when you stand up.

WARMUP EXERCISES

Collapsing

Collapsing or falling needs to be practiced slowly and from low levels until you are relaxed and know what you are doing. Generally speaking, when you fall, you land on the padded parts of the body, the buttocks, the side of the upper arm. The back rounds to absorb the shock of falling. Start your collapse from a sitting position. Try it again from a kneeling position. Start standing to see how and what you can do. When you are very sure of yourself, collapse after jumps and turns from high speeds. Avoid landing on the knee, wrist, elbow, and shoulder. If you try collapsing forward, use your hands and the bottom side of your arm, keeping your fingers together and forward, to absorb the shock. Keep your neck rigid to avoid jarring the head. Collapses can be partial (going from standing to crouching, using just the upper body) or total (from standing to lying). Work with a partner to see what kinds of partial and total collapses you can think up to do together.

PHYSICAL EXERCISES

Exercise 1— Abdomen

Position

Lie on your back on the floor, knees bent to chest, arms relaxed at the sides of the body. Lower back should be completely on the floor.

Exercise

Lower bent knees to floor until soles of feet touch floor keeping the lower back on the floor at all times. Slowly return knees to chest, again keeping the lower back on the floor. Repeat this action but each time straighten the knees a little bit until finally you are working with straight knees, keeping the lower back on the floor. This exercise gets progressively more difficult as the legs straighten. Each step should be under control before you try the next one. At any point if you feel your back coming off the floor, stop and go back to an easier position.

Suggestions

Keep the abdominal muscles as flat as you can by holding them in all the time you are working. Keep your breathing even and steady. Make sure that the lower back stays on the floor all the time you work. If it starts to come off the floor, bend your knees and slowly put your legs on the floor. Never let your legs drop to the floor out of control.

PHYSICAL EXERCISES

Exercise 2—Abdomen

Position

Lie on your back, arms stretched over head on the floor, legs together.

Exercise

Stretch arms and legs on the floor as far as you can. Now press lower back to the floor relaxing the arms and legs as you press. Repeat stretch of arms and legs, letting the back come off the floor. Repeat press of lower back to floor, relaxing arms and legs as you slide arms to side of body and legs together. Increase the pressing of the back to the floor as you slowly sit up with knees bending, soles of the feet on the floor.

Suggestions

When you press the lower back to the floor work your abdominals as hard as you can, keeping them flat and held in. When you bring your arms to the sides of your body to sit up, keep the shoulders, fingers, and neck free of tension. When you sit up do not let your feet rise off the floor.

PHYSICAL EXERCISES

Exercise 3—Abdomen

Position

Lie on your back, legs straight and together, arms close to the sides of the body.

Exercise

Tense buttock muscles hard, lift the head and feet slightly off the floor (about an inch). Make a fist with the back of the hand facing the ceiling. Beat straight up and down in small quick movements keeping arms close to the body. Continue this until abdominal muscles tire.

Suggestions

Make sure the head and feet are very close to the floor throughout the whole exercise. When you are finished, gently lower the head and feet to the floor to relax. Do not let the arms and legs drop to the floor uncontrolled. Keep the abdominal muscles flat and held in while working. Do not let them bulge.

PHYSICAL EXERCISES

Exercise 4— Abdomen

Position

Lie on your back, legs together. Straighten the knees, point the toes. Place the arms out to the sides for balance and support.

Exercise

Keep the lower back on the floor for the whole exercise. If it starts to come off the floor, stop. Raise straight legs together into the air to a right angle or as close to it as you can. Separate the legs and lower without letting them touch the floor. Bring the legs together without letting them touch the floor. Repeat the circling motion until the muscles tire. You can circle the legs clockwise and counter-clockwise.

Suggestions

Use arms out at sides for balance and support. Keep the lower back on the floor at all times. Never let the legs drop to the floor; maintain control. If the exercise is too hard, repeat exercises 1–3 until you are ready for this one. Try to keep shoulders, neck, and hands relaxed.

PHYSICAL EXERCISES

Exercise 5—Abdomen

Position

Lie on your back on the floor, arms out to the sides, legs together, toes pointed.

Exercise

Raise legs together to a right angle position in relation to the floor, keeping the lower back on the floor. Lower the legs together to the floor at side of body keeping the shoulders on the floor. Do not let the legs drop. If the shoulders start to come up from the floor, stop. Raise the legs to the right angle position and lower to other side.

Suggestions

Keep the shoulders on the floor. Never let the legs drop to the floor. Lower the legs in a slow, controlled manner, using the arms for balance and support. Keep the abdominal muscles flat, the shoulders, neck, and fingers relaxed.

PHYSICAL EXERCISES

Exercise 6—Abdomen

Position

Lie on back, arms at side of body, palms facing up. The legs are straight together, toes are pointed.

Exercise

On count one, raise the body to a semi—sitting position, knees bent, back straight, palms facing up. Hold this position for counts two and three. On count four lower the body to the floor, keeping the lower back on the floor, arms and legs relaxed. As your muscles grow stronger, try this exercise keeping the head and feet off the floor for as long as you work.

Suggestions

Try bicycling in the semi—sitting position keeping the back straight, the body lifted. Do not jerk the body to the semi—sitting position; keep the action smooth. Try to relax your neck, shoulders and fingers. Keep the abdominal muscles held in and flat. Make sure your breathing is even and steady, otherwise you will quickly find yourself out of breath.

PHYSICAL EXERCISES

Exercise 7—Shoulders

Position
Stand in the preparatory position. (See p. 18.)

Exercise
Slowly raise the shoulders as high as possible. Let the shoulders drop to a relaxed position. Repeat this a few times.

Suggestions
Keep your abodomen in, your torso lifted. Relax your arms and hands. Check fingers to get rid of accumulated tension.

PHYSICAL EXERCISES

Exercise 8—Shoulders

Position
Stand in the preparatory position.

Exercise
Move shoulders forward for two counts, then move shoulders backward as far as you can for two counts. Release the shoulders and return to preparatory position.

Suggestions
Keep your torso lifted, your hands and arms relaxed. Do not raise the shoulders as you work.

PHYSICAL EXERCISES

Exercise 9—Shoulders

Position

Stand in the preparatory position.

Exercise

Circle shoulders together, first forward then backward in a smooth, continuous action.

Suggestions

Keep the torso lifted, the abdomen in, the arms and neck relaxed. Each time return to the original position of the shoulders before circling again. Try circling one shoulder then the other in succession. Keep the action as smooth as possible.

PHYSICAL EXERCISES

Exercise 10—Back

Position
Get on your hands and knees.

Exercise
Round your back as much as you can. Do not move your shoulders. Stretch your back so that it is straight but not arched. Do this with your eyes closed so that you can feel what each position feels like.

Suggestions
Check in a mirror or work with a partner to assure that you are doing this correctly. Try rounding and straightening your back in various positions; sitting, standing, lying. Keep your abdomen in, your body relaxed.

Exercise 11—Back

Position

Stand in the preparatory position, knees slightly bent, feet slightly apart, arms relaxed at sides.

Exercise

When this exercise is done properly, the back will resemble an undulating snake. Keep the shoulders still; the knees should stay in the starting position. Start the exercise by pushing the pelvis forward as much as you can. Now rotate your pelvis so that the pelvis rolls back and the back is hyper-arched, the buttocks sticking out. Rotate the pelvis forward again and continue moving until your lower back feels tired. This is a very hard exercise to do the first few times.

Suggestions

If you can't feel your lower back, work while someone puts his hand on your lower back. Working in front of the mirror also helps. Make sure the shoulders stay loose and un-involved. Keep your stomach in, your arms and neck relaxed. If you hum while you work you will hear changes in your voice as you exercise your back. This exercise is extremely important, because it helps prevent many kinds of back trouble and also helps relieve body tension.

PHYSICAL EXERCISES

Exercise 12—Back

Position

Sit on the floor, knees straight, legs together and extended in front of you.

Exercise

Sitting very lifted, raise both arms at your sides slowly. Keeping your shoulders down, lift the arms until they are extended overhead. Work with a partner or a mirror to make sure your back stays straight. In the beginning this may be quite hard and you will find you are rounding your back without knowing it.

Suggestions

Try this exercise with the legs as far apart as you can put them without strain. Let the little toe be as close to the floor as you can put it without strain. This insures the leg being in the proper position. Keep the knees straight. When the whole foot is working the toes are pointed. To relax your back, bend your knees and round your back. Gently bob a few times.

PHYSICAL EXERCISES

Exercise 13—Back

Position

Sit on the floor, knees straight, legs together, and arms relaxed at sides of body.

Exercise

Round the back and slowly lower it to the floor until the small of the back is in contact with the floor. Keeping the legs on the floor at all times, straighten the back and rise to the original position.

Suggestions

Keep the shoulders and neck relaxed. The legs should be working hard. This means the knees are very straight, the toes pointed. If you are having trouble feeling whether or not your back is working properly, look in a mirror, work with a friend, or put your hand on the small of the back to help you feel what should be working. Keep your torso lifted, your abdomen in, your breath even and relaxed. As a variation, try doing this exercise with the feet apart. See exercise 12, (p. 38) for proper use of legs in this position.

PHYSICAL EXERCISES

Exercise 14—Back

Position
Lie on stomach, arms extended over head, legs together out straight.

Exercise
Gradually raise the arms, head and legs as high as you can in two counts. Lower to starting position in two counts. Repeat the exercise in four counts making sure to take four full counts to return to original position.

Suggestions
As you move the body up and down, stretch the arms and legs out. Lift the head and try to keep the shoulders from hunching up. Move on all the counts keeping the movement steady and smooth.

PHYSICAL EXERCISES

Exercise 15—Back

Position

Lie on the stomach, arms extended over head, legs extended out straight and together.

Exercise

Raise the head and legs off the floor leaving the hands on the floor. Kick the legs up and down as in flutter-kicking in swimming. Try to keep the thighs off the floor.

Suggestions

This exercise will probably hurt your pelvic bones if you work on a bare floor. Try doing it with a flat pad or cushion underneath your pelvic bones. Raise the head and the legs off the floor without straining the neck. Keep the legs extended as you kick. The span of the kick should be about six inches.

PHYSICAL EXERCISES

Exercise 16—Back

Position

Stand in the preparatory position with the feet quite wide apart.

Exercise

This exercise is the back bend but it should be learned in stages. Never do more than you can do with control. Do not use aids, like a wall. Work slowly and carefully. Start by putting one arm in front of you. Bend your knees and swing the other arm over your head and behind you. Go only as far as you can control. Repeat using other arm. Each time you work, go a little further until you can touch the floor. When you can touch the floor with each arm and can get up easily, you are ready to try swinging both arms over head and behind you until they are touching the floor. Get up by swinging one arm in front of you, return to starting position.

Suggestions

After you have tried this for a few times, relax your back by bending over at the waist and bob a bit. Keep the soles of your feet flat on the floor while you are working. Keep your torso lifted, your neck, shoulders, and hands relaxed.

PHYSICAL EXERCISES

Exercise 17—Head and Neck

Position
Stand in the preparatory position.

Exercise
Circle head to the side, back, other side, and then to the front. Repeat, going in the other direction.

Suggestions
To start, drop head as far to each direction as you can. The neck muscles should feel stretched. If you get dizzy, stop. Focus sharply on a specific point. Keep the torso lifted, the abdomen in.

PHYSICAL EXERCISES

Exercise 18—Head and Neck

Position

This exercise can be done in any relaxed position.

Exercise

Tense all the facial muscles. Then let the tension ebb away. Check to make sure there is no residual tension around the eyes and nose. Experiment with tensing part of the face, relaxing the other.

Suggestions

Our facial muscles are in constant use. When we are tense, it is reflected in our face. The next time you know you are worried or upset, see what happens if you consciously try to relax the facial muscles.

PHYSICAL EXERCISES

Exercise 19—Arms and Hands

Position

Stand in the preparatory position.

Exercise

Raise the arms out to the sides with great tension, stopping just below shoulder level. Release the tension and let the arms drop, falling where they will. Experiment, first letting the palms lead, then the fingers, etc.

Suggestions

If you let the arms drop without directing them they will probably slap your thighs. This is what should happen. The harder the slap, the more relaxed your arms are. Watch that you do not tense the rest of your body. Keep the lift in the torso.

PHYSICAL EXERCISES

Exercise 20—Arms and Hands

Position
Stand in the preparatory position.

Exercise
Bring the hands to the front of the body at waist level and circle wrists one way, then the other. After circling in both directions shake out the wrists. Make the shaking motion as small and as fast as you can.

Suggestions
Check alignment. Wrists should describe a full circle without the arm moving.

PHYSICAL EXERCISES

Exercise 21—Arms and Hands

Position
Stand in the preparatory position.

Exercise
Bring the right arm up directly front until it is straight overhead, letting the back of the hand lead. Return to original position, letting the heel of the hand lead. Repeat using other arm. Repeat using both arms together.

Suggestions
Keep arms relaxed and light in feeling. Keep the shoulders down. Keep your torso lifted, your abdomen in. Use your arms to the front and to the side. Think of feeling air.

PHYSICAL EXERCISES

Exercise 22—Arms and hands

Position
Stand in the preparatory position.

Exercise
Swing the right arm across your body, then swing it out to the side. Now swing it around in a full circle and finish by swinging your arm out to the side. Repeat this using your left arm. Now use both arms together, starting first with the arms out to the sides. Repeat, starting with arms crossed in front of the body. The pattern will always be swing, swing, circle, swing. When you feel ready, bend the knees with each swing.

Suggestions
Keep the swing relaxed, the body lifted, and the abdomen in.

PHYSICAL EXERCISES

Exercise 23—Legs

Position

Stand in the preparatory position.

Exercise

Place hands on the upper thighs so that the thumbs touch each other slightly. Tighten the buttocks muscles and turn the thighs out so that the fingers can no longer touch each other. The knee should be directly over the big toe. It prevents the knee from bending over the instep, a very weak position, causing bad alignment. When you can feel the thighs working properly do this exercise without using your fingers. Bend the knees a bit and see if you can still keep the knees over the big toes. Move in various positions, keeping the knees over the big toes.

Suggestions

Make certain that you are able to feel the muscle action involved in keeping the big toe under the knee before you do jumps or leaps. This is part of improving your kinesthetic sense. Keep the rest of the body in good alignment.

PHYSICAL EXERCISES

Exercise 24—Legs

Position
Stand in the preparatory position.

Exercise
Keep the knees over the big toes throughout the entire exercise. Bend the knees slowly and feel the tension in the thighs as if you were pulling the inner thighs together without moving them together. Now straighten the knees in three counts and feel as if you are pushing the legs apart as the knees straighten. Keep the heels on the floor the whole time and bend your knees as much as you can without lifting your heels off the floor.

Suggestions
Keep the body erect, letting only the legs work. Keep the abdomen in, the shoulders, neck, and fingers free of tension. Do this exercise in a mirror or with a friend to make sure your body does not tilt. When you can do this exercise, increase the count, keeping the heels on the floor as long as you can. Try this exercise with the heels touching each other as long as you can keep them together.

PHYSICAL EXERCISES

Exercise 25—Legs

Position

Lie on your back, arms at the sides of your body, legs extended and together.

Exercise

Raise the right leg up as high as you can, keeping the knee straight, the toes pointed. When the leg is up as far as it can go, flex (bend) the right ankle and the right knee, keeping the sole of the foot parallel to the ceiling. Without moving the thigh, straighten the leg. Repeat the flexing and extending until the leg begins to tremble. Lower the right leg gently and repeat the exercise using the left leg. Repeat the exercise using both legs together. Lower both legs to the floor, keeping the lower back on the floor. If the lower back starts to come off the floor, bend the knees and gently put the feet on the floor.

Suggestions

Work the leg on the floor by keeping the knees and toes as extended as possible. When you flex the knee and ankle of the leg in the air, be sure to keep the sole of the foot facing the ceiling and the thigh still.

PHYSICAL EXERCISES

Exercise 26—Legs

Position

Stand in the preparatory position with the right leg extended in front of you, with the foot slightly off the ground.

Exercise

Sit, without using the hands, keeping the right leg extended in front of you. Stand, without using the hands, still keeping the right leg extended in front of you. Repeat, using left leg.

Suggestions

If you are having trouble standing, you can get extra momentum by swinging the leg over your head, then standing quickly as you swing it in to the extended position in front of you. Swing your arms forward as you stand for extra momentum.

PHYSICAL EXERCISES

Exercise 27—Legs

Position

Stand in preparatory position, feet facing forward, with right toe touching the floor, the right heel off the floor.

Exercise

Proper use of the feet is essential to avoid injury. It is especially necessary when working on cold or non-resilient floors, such as concrete. The proper sequence in using the feet is: toe (for an instant), ball of foot (metatarsal), heel of foot, then the bend of the knee. Each time you jump or leap the heel must touch the floor before the knee bends. Use this exercise to warm up your feet before you jump, leap, or run.

At the start, only the right toe is touching the floor. Now place the ball of the foot on the floor, then the heel. Finally, bend the knee and shift the weight so that the right foot is on the floor and the left foot is off the floor, except for the toe, which is resting lightly on the floor. Repeat this exercise slowly until you are sure of the sequence. Gradually increase your speed until you can do this prancing moving across the room.

Suggestions

Work slowly and carefully. Watch your alignment. Try doing this exercise forwards, backwards, and in a circle.

PHYSICAL EXERCISES

Exercise 28—Legs

Position
Stand in the preparatory position.

Exercise
Raise arms up to below shoulder level and slightly forward. Lift the right leg in front of you slightly off the floor with the knee straight and toe extended. Repeat this three more times, bringing the leg slightly higher each time. Try to reach a right angle or higher. Repeat this exercise using the left leg. Repeat this exercise lifting the leg to the side, then to the back.

Suggestions
When you raise the knee to the side do it first with the knee facing the ceiling, then with the side of the knee facing the ceiling. Keep the body quiet; do not lean forward or backward to get the leg higher. Keep the torso lifted, the legs very extended, the fingers, neck, and shoulders relaxed.

PHYSICAL EXERCISES

Exercise 29—Legs

Position

Stand against a flat wall.

Exercise

Slowly begin to sit but stop when your thighs are parallel to the floor, your legs at right angles to your thighs. Stay in this position for thirty seconds, increasing to two minutes as your muscles get stronger. Keep your arms and hands relaxed, your breathing even.

Suggestions

Try to keep your legs as relaxed as possible. This means that you must work to eliminate all unnecessary tension. When you have finished the exercise stretch your legs fully and carefully avoiding sharp, straining motion. Singing while you work helps.

PHYSICAL EXERCISES

Exercise 30—Legs

Position

Stand in the preparatory position.

Exercise

Bend the knees, keeping the legs together until the heels start to come off the floor. Keeping the weight back, gradually increase the bend until you are on your knees. Do not flop to your knees. If you lack the strength to maintain control, use your hands to absorb the shock. Never bang your knees to the floor under any condition. When you are on your knees, keep your back lifted and your head in line with your back. Gradually, lower your body to the floor. Go only as far as you can control. Eventually you ought to be able to go all the way to the floor and rise, with control. Make sure the insteps are flat on the floor before you start lowering your body to the floor.

Suggestions

When you lower your body to the floor, keep your arms out in front of you for balance. Do not let the body curve. This puts strain on the lower back. The thighs should do all the work. When you are confident you can try jumping or running into it.

PHYSICAL EXERCISES

Exercise 31—Total Body

Position

Stand in the preparatory position with arms clasped behind head, chin touching chest.

Exercise

This exercise helps relieve accumulated tension along the spinal column and also helps to stretch the backs of the legs, increasing flexibility. Lift the torso and, maintaining the lift, bend the body over as far as it will go. Keep the chin touching the chest throughout the entire exercise. When you cannot bend any further, release the arms and let them drop down. Keeping the fingers relaxed, slowly rise. As you rise stretch the back as if you were pushing against an imaginary weight. Rise to standing position, lift the shoulders up and around, then down. You should be in the preparatory position when you finish.

Suggestions

This is a good exercise to do when you are tense, have sore muscles, or want to increase your stretch in the back of the legs. Make sure the chin stays in contact with the chest and that you keep lifting. Keep the abdomen in, the weight on the balls of the feet.

PHYSICAL EXERCISES

Exercise 32—Total Body

Position
Stand in the preparatory position.

Exercise
Circle the head around, starting front, then side, back, other side, and front. Repeat to the other direction. Keep the shoulders and the rest of the body still. Repeat, using head and shoulders, keeping the rest of the body lifted. Repeat to other side. Keeping the arms relaxed, circle the head, shoulders, and torso to each side. As you develop strength, add the arms by keeping them extended overhead (shoulders down). Try it to each side with legs bent, using good alignment.

Suggestions
Each time you change direction, focus on a specific point to avoid dizziness. Remember to keep the body lifted, the abdomen in, the shoulders down. Divide the weight evenly on the ball of each foot. Be careful when you start to use the arms because they increase the amount of weight on the torso. If you keep your body lifted there will not be too much weight on the small of the back.

PHYSICAL EXERCISES

Exercise 33—Total Body

Position
Stand in the preparatory position.

Exercise
Warm up feet. (See Exercise 26, p. 52.) Jump eight small jumps with the heels together, the toes apart. Make sure that the heels touch the floor on every jump. Bend the knees as you land. Repeat the jumps with the feet apart. Combine these two so that you do sixteen jumps, alternating feet together, then apart.

Suggestions
Check in the mirror to make sure that you stay lifted. The body should not shift weight forward or backward as you jump. Keep the abdomen in, the shoulders, neck, and fingers relaxed. Gradually increase the size of your jumps, maintaining good alignment.

PHYSICAL EXERCISES

Exercise 34—Total Body

Position
Stand in the preparatory position.

Exercise
Raise the arms forward, keeping the shoulders down. Swing the arms and upper body to the floor, bending the knees as you continue the arm swing. At this point the body is in a right angle position with the arms behind. Reverse the swing, bending and straightening the knees as you did before. End up with the arms overhead, the body straight. Repeat the swing several times. As a variation, try jumping up as you swing up. Then jump, concentrating and focusing on the downward movement. Work for a relaxed and easy rhythm.

Suggestions
Maintain good alignment, keep the body lifted and relaxed. When you add the jumps make sure the heels touch the floor after each jump. Keep all the movements relaxed.

PHYSICAL EXERCISES

Exercise 35—Total Body

Position

Stand in the preparatory position. Extend the arms out to the side, just below the shoulder level, slightly front of center and slightly rounded.

Exercise

Keep both legs straight throughout the exercise. Extend the right leg back, pointing the toes. Keep the back lifted as you lower the body. The back leg will come off the ground. Take four counts to do this. Keep the head in line with the rest of the body. Place hands on the ground and try to lift the back leg higher, four times. Keeping the back lifted. return to starting position. Repeat the exercise using the other leg.

Suggestions

Keep the torso lifted, the shoulders down and relaxed. Move the body as if it were one piece. Fix your eyes on a non-moving object to help maintain balance.

PHYSICAL EXERCISES

Exercise 36—Total Body

Position

Stand in the preparatory position, arms out to side just below shoulder level, slightly rounded.

Exercise

Tilt body to left, extend right leg out and lift for four counts. Bend supporting leg and round body, bringing the extended leg in close. Slowly extend body and return to starting position. Repeat to other side. Try doing this with the leg extended to the back and then to the front. Always work both legs equally.

Suggestions

Focus on a non-moving spot for balance. Keep the body lifted. Experiment with varying dynamics. Keep the abdomen in, the weight on the balls of the feet.

PHYSICAL EXERCISES

Relaxation

This exercise cannot be done quickly. For best results you should work in a quiet room with no interruptions. It is a good exercise to do if you are tired and have no time to take a nap. It is not an easy exercise to do. When you tense one side of the body, the other side usually tenses too. If you concentrate on what you are doing, however, you will be able to effect the desired tension, thus greatly increasing your body control.

The principle involved in this exercise is to work a muscle group very hard, then let go. This is achieved by consciously letting the muscles you have just worked go limp so that there is a feeling of heaviness and inertia. The following relaxation exercise should be learned and practiced regularly as part of your daily exercise program. Like any skill, the more you work at it, the more successful you will be.

Read the exercise through once or twice until you understand what you will be doing. Lie down and reread it so that you can try part or all of it without the book in your hand. Although you will not be able to go into a deep state of tranquility the first time, you will be able to eventually, with enough practice.

PHYSICAL EXERCISE

Exercise 37—Relaxation

Lie down on your back, put a small pillow under your knees if you are more comfortable this way, and loosen any tight or restrictive clothing. Turn your head slightly to one side and let your arms and hands assume a position that is natural for them. Whatever position you take, take the same one each time you practice — head turned the same way, arms in the same place, et cetera.

Tense your right leg, including toes, ankle, knee, and thigh as hard as you can. Hold this tension for a few seconds, then go limp. Do not move the right leg after it has become limp and heavy. Now try the left leg. Tense the toes, knee, and thigh. Hold the tension, then release it, letting the entire leg get heavy and limp. Concentrate on what you are doing so that you do not move either leg as you continue to work. Tense the stomach muscles and chest muscles as hard as you can, then release. Tense your right arm, fingers, forearm, upper arm. Release the tension. Repeat, using left arm and taking care not to move the right arm. Keeping both arms quiet, tense your shoulders as hard as you can. Hold the tension, then release. Repeat using the neck muscles. Now work with your facial muscles around the eyes, nose, mouth, and forehead. Let go, checking each area to make sure there is no residual tension. Breathe so that there is a long inhalation followed by an exhalation that seems to come by itself. Feel all the tension and tightness ooze from your body. You should feel completely limp, heavy, and inert, totally at peace. Stay this way for at least five minutes; use a timer if necessary. Terminate the exercise by putting your arms over your head on the floor, and stretching your whole body as hard as you can; then get up. If you are doing this exercise before going to sleep at night, do not stretch.

While working on this exercise it is very important that you concentrate on what you are doing rather than on extraneous problems. If you really work on this exercise you will not be able to think about anything else. Being able to use your tension rather than being at the mercy of it is necessary to get rid of extra tension. You should make sure that you do this exercise when you are very tired or very busy. This is when you need it most.

PHYSICAL EXERCISES

Exercise 38—Relaxation

Position

This exercise can be done in any position, lying, sitting, or standing.

Exercise

In whatever position you are working, try to release the hands so they are as loose as possible. Let the head fall so that the neck is not supporting it. Watch your breathing for a few seconds. Now increase the span of the inhalation and let the exhalation happen by itself. Exhalation is a relaxation of the breathing muscles. Keep this pattern of long inhalation followed by the exhalation. This is the breathing pattern of sleep. Concentrate only on the breathing, nothing else. When you are ready to work stretch as fully as you can, your whole body. You will probably yawn a few times, but this is natural.

Suggestions

This exercise is very good for actors to do just before going on stage. It helps to remove the extra tension that inhibits good performance. It is much better than pacing, which only serves to increase tension.

CHAPTER THREE

EXPLORING SPACE

These groups of exercises are planned to give the actor the opportunity to combine imagination with what he has learned about muscle control in the physical exercises. It is more difficult to maintain this control while moving across the floor than while working in place. For example, it is more difficult to walk correctly than it is to stand correctly. It is especially hard for those who are still self-conscious about their appearance.

These exercises to explore space are based on the primary patterns that human beings use to move from one place to another. These primary patterns are: walking, running, jumping, hopping, creeping, and crawling. The actor must learn to use these patterns to explore extremes of movement. The actor cannot be satisfied to know that he can leap. He must also know how high he can leap. Even more important, he must know how much higher it is possible for him to leap if he tries. A singer can reach high C comfortably only if she has reached high D or E in practice. Therefore, it is the purpose of these exercises to provide a concrete method for an actor to push himself beyond self-imposed limitations. When an actor is conditioned for greater demands, ordinary demands can be easily met.

Another purpose of these exercises is to teach the actor how to move safely, how to be prepared to handle accidental problems like falling from a stage, or a ladder. An actor needs to be trained to work with limited or no peripheral vision so that he can work with a mask and not fear falling off edges. If the actor learns to use an inner focus, he will not fear whirling around on the stage if his part should call for this. If the following questions can be answered with a yes, the actor should be able to move with reasonable safety on stage or in any acting area:

1. Can I run fast within a small space and come to a quick, safe, stop?
2. Can I run and then jump without stopping the momentum?
3. Can I fall on the floor after jumping or turning without being afraid that I will hurt myself?
4. Can I move backwards comfortably with a sense of where I am?
5. Can I turn and swirl with ease, finding my focus when I stop?
6. Can I leap or turn with my face toward the ceiling knowing how much space I can use safely?
7. Can I move quickly and safely in a room filled with many obstacles?

These are only a few challenges the actor can pose for himself. The more he works, the more ideas he will discover. Besides providing a means to go beyond self-imposed limitations, these exercises will help actors who have coordination problems. If a person is poorly coordinated he will generally appear to be awkward on stage. Although some coordination problems are complex and deep-rooted, an actor can appear to be relaxed, well—coordinated, and graceful by training his kinesthetic sense and reinforcing basic movement patterns. For example, most people walk with the left leg and swing their right arm forward without thinking about it. This is called opposition and it results in a kind of balance. Try walking with the right foot forward and swing the right arm forward, then the left arm and leg. See how strange it feels. The same idea of balance applies to slightly more complex patterns: Skip, leap, step-hop, and slide. When you are doing these exercises always remember to use your feet correctly by landing on the ball of the foot, then the heel, and finally bending your knee. When you jump or leap in the air you do use your toes as you land but only for an instant. To increase jumping height make sure that you stretch your foot in the air and point your toes. This gives you increased lift-off power. Always work by starting out easily and carefully. There is danger of injury if you do not warm your muscles before working on strenuous exercises. This is particularly true if you work on a concrete floor, in a cold room, or on a cold floor. If you have not been working for a while, be extra careful that your enthusiasm for working does not lead to impulsive leaps that your body is not ready for. Pay attention to your own body so that you do not change from a relaxed pace to a more strenuous one until you are really ready.

Experiment with speed, doing these patterns both slowly and quickly, smoothly and erratically. Be loose or tense, quiet or full of sound. Actually use your voice although specific words are not necessary. Try the movement patterns while holding hands with a partner or engaging in kinds of physical contact. Try the same movement patterns using emotional contact only. Through emotional contact those watching, as well as those moving, sense a connection, even though there may be no physical contact. Be sure to use your arms, head, and torso in many different ways to increase the variety of possibilities.

BASIC MOVEMENT PATTERNS

Exercise 1—Run. . .Jump

Purpose
To change directions without losing momentum and control.

Exercise
Run. . .jump.

Suggestions
Try this forward, then backward. Make different floor patterns, such as circles, squares, and triangles. Work on your toes, as high as you can. Move with bent knees as low to the ground as is possible still keeping the basic pattern of run and jump. Remember a jump means taking off into the air with two feet and landing on two feet. A hop uses only one foot. Try working with a partner and see how this affects your possibilities. Try jumping with the emphasis and focus on the downward movement. Try jumping with your face in the air or looking down to the floor. Try jumping with a changing focus.

BASIC MOVEMENT PATTERNS

Exercise 2—Run. . .Jump – Turn

Purpose
To change directions in the air without losing balance and momentum.

Exercise
Run. . .Jump – Turn

Suggestions
Try this exercise moving backward and forward. See what happens when you use your arms to help keep your balance. How does the balance change if you do not use your arms? Vary this exercise by doing it with bent knees, staying as close to the floor as possible. How many ways can you find to jump, then turn? Do the sequence of run–jump–turn several times, without stopping, to practice balance.

BASIC MOVEMENT PATTERNS

Exercise 3—Run. . .Jump — Turn. . .Fall

Purpose

To change energy levels, direction, and speed with ease and control.

Exercise

Run. . .Jump—Turn. . .Fall.

Suggestions

Practice falling, starting from a low position, until you feel sure of yourself. Remember to land in a rounded position on the back of the hip or shoulder. Avoid using your hands to help you. Never land on your knee, elbow, or wrist. Try this exercise slowly at first, then work up to as great a speed as you can manage with control. See if you can repeat this exercise without stopping so that you get up from the fall very quickly and start again. This exercise can be done backward and sideways. Try using your voice when you fall or turn, and work for as many effects as you can. See what happens if you work with a partner or in a group.

BASIC MOVEMENT PATTERNS

Exercise 4—Run. . .Jump – Turn. . .Fall. . .Roll

Purpose
To change direction, speed, level, and balance with ease and control.

Exercise
Run. . .Jump–Turn. . .Fall. . .Roll.

Suggestions
This exercise should be practiced as smoothly as possible. If you have enough room to work in, try doing the whole sequence three or four times without stopping. Try doing it in a circle as well as in a straight line. Try getting up from the roll in many different ways. Try working with someone close behind you so that you have to work very quickly. Use your voice in different ways. Imagine different situations that would cause you to move in a variety of ways. Work with people coming at you from different angles. How does this affect your physical activity or emotional state?

Rolling and falling in quick succession

BASIC MOVEMENT PATTERNS

Exercise 5—Creeping

Purpose
To explore primitive locomotive patterns.

Exercise
Creep.

Suggestions
When you creep, you use your hands and knees. Be careful if you are working on a concrete floor or if you have bad knees. This is one of the earliest locomotive patterns of humans. While you creep notice how it makes you feel. Try working in opposition (left hand, right leg) as well as with the same arm and leg. Which feels more comfortable? Keep most of the weight on your hands. How many ways can you find to creep? What kinds of vocal sounds can you make? When you work with a partner what kinds of variations can you make?

BASIC MOVEMENT PATTERNS

Exercise 6—Crawling

Purpose
To explore and use primitive locomotive patterns.

Exercise
Crawl.

Suggestions
When you crawl you use your hands and feet but your knees are off the ground. Does crawling make you feel different from creeping? Which pattern makes you feel more mobile? Try crawling using just your toes or just your heels. Try crawling as various animals might. Try working backwards and sideways. See how much space you can make your body use. Try arching your back. Work with legs straight as well as bent. Work very quickly as well as very slowly. See how many sounds you can make. Work first very relaxed, then very tense. Try crawling with a partner on your back. Try creating different situations which would require you to crawl.

Using space economically in a group creep

This next set of exercises is arranged to give the actors an opportunity to create movement patterns of their own. Preconceived ideas such as ''I will move arrogantly like a queen,'' or ''I will crawl like a caterpillar,'' should be avoided. This leads to cliche. Try the exercises and let the emotion or feelings develop from the movements. You will find this method an effective way of stimulating emotion. It may not happen the first time; but if you concentrate and repeat the sequence several times you will find an attitude directing your energy. Be demanding of yourself and observe what you do and how you do it. Avoid repetition. You will probably become sweaty and dirty, but these are signs of real involvement. Work carefully. Do not rush to a finish. Let the others wait. Reflect on each new sensory experience whether it occurs in a movement class, walking at night in the spring, or wriggling your toes in the mud. Hang on to the memories of these new experiences and use them to recreate certain feelings. Analyze the limitations you have encountered in your movement work. Repeat the physical exercises that strengthen your weaknesses. The more you expect of yourself, the more you will be able to do and the more you will want to do. Be sensitive to the others in your class and give them support. Do not laugh at clumsy attempts. Offer to help with a movement that you can do but which a fellow actor finds more difficult. More learning and experimentation can take place in an atmoshpere of cooperation.

Complex Movement Patterns

Complex movement patterns consist of movements which combine several basic patterns. Listed below are the complex patterns used in the exercises, and their descriptions:

LEAP
This is an extended run. The weight shifts from one foot to the other. Leaps can be done for height or for distance, depending on the thrust of the energy.

STEP—HOP
When you step-hop, the foot pattern is step right, hop right; step left, hop left. There is no weight change on a hop.

SKIP
This is a step-hop with no pause after the hop.

SLIDE
This foot pattern is step right, bring the left foot to the right foot, then step right again. (Step—together—step). When you do this sideways it is a slide. When it is done with the body facing forward, it becomes a gallop.

Any combination of the preceding complex movement patterns can be done in many ways. Regardless of the variation, be sure to use your feet properly. Work with your torso both lifted and bent. Use your head and arms purposefully. Know what they are doing at all times. There is great joy to be found in moving for your own pleasure. It comes from being able to let go and at the same time knowing you can control what you are doing. See if you can sing or shout at the top of your lungs while you are leaping and jumping around the room. If you can do this comfortably you are on the way to enjoying what you are and what you can do in movement.

Learning to move together in a single direction-(group skip)

COMPLEX MOVEMENT PATTERNS

Exercise 1—Run. . .Run. . .Leap

Purpose
To improve coordination and learn to leap for distance and for height.

Exercise
Run. . . Run. . .Leap

Suggestions
The foot pattern should change each time so that you get a chance to leap on each foot (right—left—right; left—right—left). Try leaping with your arms and face lifted to the ceiing. Vary the leap by focusing on the floor. A leap for distance uses the thrust of energy in a forward manner. In a leap for height, the energy thrust is upward. See how many ways you can change your use of arms and feet to create new kinds of leaps. Experiment with the use of the voice so that you shout at the peak of the leap, as you begin or as you end. How does the placement or variety of sound affect your movement? Try just running any number of runs before you leap. Is this easier than two runs and a leap? Why? Try leaping with a partner to explore variety.

COMPLEX MOVEMENT PATTERNS

Exercise 2—Step–Hop

Purpose
To improve coordination, create new ways to use the body while doing a step–hop.

Exercise
Step–Hop.

Suggestions
Try this with the free leg (leg with no weight on it) extended to the front. Keep the supporting leg (leg with weight on it) bent. What happens to your balance and control when you extend the free leg to the side or to the back? Can you extend your leg so that the knee is absolutely straight, toes pointed? Work with a partner and see what variations you can create. Remember to keep your torso lifted all the time unless you are purposefully doing a variation.

Learning to move in space with a partner

COMPLEX MOVEMENT PATTERNS

Exercise 3—Skip

Purpose
To improve coordination and to practice proper use of the feet.

Exercise
Skip.

Suggestions
Make sure that the heels touch the floor each time you land, unless you are purposefully doing a variation. This ensures proper use of the feet but also helps develop thrust for the next skip so you can go higher into the air. Placing the heels on the floor also helps give you a sense of balance and placement. Try various kinds of skips such as low, high, tense, or relaxed. Change the floor pattern so that you go sideways or backward, in a circle or in an irregular design. Skip with great abandon, with a partner or with a group. Try humming; let the sound change as your body moves.

COMPLEX MOVEMENT PATTERNS

Exercise 4—Slide

Purpose
To improve coordination, use of feet and sense of timing.

Exercise
Slide.

Suggestions
Slide four times to one side, four times to the other side without stopping the movement, continuing in the same forward direction. Repeat doing only two slides. Try it with a partner working face to face and then back to back. Be sure to use your feet precisely and cleanly. See how many variations of your own you can work out.

EXPLORATION OF EXTREMES OF MOVEMENT

The following exercises are all planned to increase the ability to explore, and extend one's sense of space. If you use the diagonal of a room you usually have the most area to work. In addition, particularly on a wooden floor, you will have more traction because you work against the grain. Give yourself enough space to move by waiting until the person in front of you has finished or is well out of your way. While you are waiting for your turn, do not crowd the person who is waiting for his turn to move. Use the time to observe your fellow students and to prepare yourself physically and mentally for your own turn.

You will find some exercises that use the term explode. The word is used here to mean a sudden release of energy without prior anticipation. None of the preceding movements should indicate what is going to happen. There should be no "telegraphing" of the message. You can change the kind of exploding by varying the initial energy thrust. For example, you can start with the torso, the arms, or the legs, however you feel the impulse. Even if you have to work at it, try to approach the movement differently each time so that you get varied kinds of feelings and attitudes about what you are doing. If you doubt your results, ask your fellow students what you look like. You can explode up in the air, down to the ground, or to the side. Once you start you will be able to think of many possibilities. Try working with one or more partners. This will change the stimulation and alter the affects.

EXPLORATION OF EXTREMES OF MOVEMENT

Exercise 1—Using space

Purpose

To explore how much space one can use to move in.

Exercise

Reach out and stretch. While moving across the floor ''feel'' as much space as you can, as if there are invisible walls and you are trying to see how wide, high, and long they are.

Suggestions

Use your arms fully extended, fingers working. Use your legs as if they are arms. Keep your torso strong and lifted to support what your arms and legs are doing.

EXPLORATION OF EXTREMES OF MOVEMENT

Exercise 2—Defining Space

Purpose
To articulate movement in space.

Exercise
Define your reaching, as in the previous exercise, by moving in large circles, turning in place, going to one side then to the other. Take large steps in between the turns so that you progress forward.

Suggestions
Work on toes, using your body in a lifted manner. Start from a squat position and keep your turns as close to the floor as you can. If you keep losing your balance, it may be because you are not using your torso for support. Try to focus on a specific point as you work and it may help you to maintain your balance.

EXPLORATION OF EXTREMES OF MOVEMENT

Exercise 3—Using the floor

Purpose
To explore movement possibilities using the floor for support.

Exercise
Go across the floor, keeping as much contact with it as you can.

Suggestions
See how many ways you can use the floor, besides the conventional method of creeping or crawling. Try slithering, keeping your torso off the ground, using your feet and fingers for support. How can you use your hair or head to create unusual movement? Use sounds to help. Try working with a partner or a group.

Exploring levels in group crawl

EXPLORATION OF EXTREMES OF MOVEMENT

Exercise 4—Exploding

Purpose
To be able to release energy yet maintain control.

Exercise
Explode in the air, then relax into a partial collapse.

Suggestions
Repeat the sequence several times so that you can practice maintaining your energy between the times you explode. Keep the movement going across the floor regardless of what you do. Use your voice in different ways. Work with a partner. You can use a scarf to help maintain contact in the beginning. See how the impulse to explode differs if your partner works with you or in opposition to you. See how many times it takes you before you feel that you have gone as high or as low as you can. The more you work at this, the easier it will become.

EXPLORATION OF EXTREMES OF MOVEMENT

Exercise 5—Swirling

Purpose

To relax yet maintain balance while turning.

Exercise

Swirl across the floor going to each side. Start from various positions and let the force of the swing move your arms. The swing should last only as long as the momentum. Then, start again to the other side.

Suggestions

Those watching the actor swirl should get a feeling of euphoria, joy, and release. If you have trouble maintaining your balance, focus sharply on a point when you stop swinging. Do not let the energy die between turns. Experiment with all kinds of ways to use your torso, arms, and head. Change tempos and vocal sounds for variation.

EXPLORATION OF EXTREMES OF MOVEMENT

Exercise 6—Inner focus

Purpose

To learn to develop a sense of inner focus.

Exercise

Focus on a fixed spot straight ahead of you. Close your eyes and walk toward it. Repeat the same thing working backward and sideways.

Suggestions

Work very slowly in the beginning. When you feel competent, vary your speeds. Mark out a line so you can see your deviation. Have a person at either end to prevent you from hitting anything. Try working at different levels (crouching, tip-toes, etc.) How does this effect your accuracy? Use your voice to make sounds, recite speeches, or give directions. You can also make the focal point a sound by closing your eyes and moving toward a sound source.

EXPLORATION OF EXTREMES OF MOVEMENT

Exercise 7—Walking with head circling.

Purpose
to improve coordination and balance and to learn to use inner focus.

Exercise
Walk forward in a straight line. Circle the head, at the same time keeping the circling motion smooth and unaccented.

Suggestions
Work along an actual line if possible so that you are able to see deviation. Focus on a spot before you start and try to maintain this focus inside your head as you continue. Circle your head to each side. Try working backwards and sideways. Try to talk as you work. Try working with your eyes closed. How does this affect your balance? This exercise requires great concentration and if you feel as if you are getting tired, stop and do something else requiring less concentration.

EXPLORATION OF EXTREMES OF MOVEMENT

Exercise 8—Forward and backward rolls to stand.

Purpose
To improve coordination, balance, and to learn to move quickly in space without fear.

Exercise
Do a series of rolls, both forward and backward, and come to a standing position. Stand completely still focusing on a fixed spot. When you do the rolls make sure your chin stays on your chest, the fingers are together, the hands forward. Try coming to a stand on one leg. Try using your voice to make sounds. Try using real words when you stand up to see if you can maintain your balance when your concentration is divided. You should work on mats or mattresses where possible. If this is not possible and you want to try the exercise, wear padded clothing and work very carefully. When you have learned to feel comfortable doing this exercise you have learned a very important safety skill. Try working very quickly or very slowly.

EXPLORATION OF EXTREMES OF MOVEMENT

Exercise 9—Working with obstacles.

Purpose

To learn to work around obstacles with ease and control, and to improve coordination.

Exercise

Fill the working space with any kind of obstacles that you can find such as chairs, desks, chalk, material, sticks, etc. Move in and around them with varying rates of speed. Try to jump over some, on top of others, or even under where possible.

Suggestions

Set up situations such as being chased, playing tag, or being drunk. Avoid bumping into objects, or other movement that is not purposeful. Work with little or no light when you are sure you know the room. Change the placement of the objects to see if you can still work with control. Working like this will enable you to work with greater ease on a crowded stage.

EXPLORATION OF EXTREMES OF MOVEMENT

Exercise 10—Fast movement and sudden stops

Purpose
To develop the concept of center, to improve coordination, and to use inner focus.

Exercise
Move in place using as much space as possible. Have someone clap or make a sharp sound. As soon as you hear the sound, freeze. Try again, increase the tempo of your movements. Use inner focus to stop without wobbling. When you feel ready, cover distance.

Suggestions
Try to feel a sense of center, of balance, that makes it possible for you to be on one foot yet feel perfectly stable. Work with a partner and then in a group. Use sounds that stop with your freeze or that start after the freeze. Vary the length of time you work before freezing. Work to a sight signal rather thán a sound signal. Explore how many different levels you can work on. (Tip-toe, crawling, etc.)

Finding a center of balance while working off-center

CHAPTER FOUR

EXPLORING NON-VERBAL COMMUNICATION

The exercises in non-verbal communication are designed to prepare the actor to work with imagination, flexibility, and confidence, so that he can approach any role with the knowledge that his body is ready to work. These exercises are aimed toward exploration of movement communication without concentration on the creation of specific roles.

These exercises in non-verbal communication should be done with one partner, with two or three, and with the whole group. See what you need to do in order to establish emotional rather than physical contact. When working with physical contact do not limit your exploration to the use of your hands. Take the time to go beyond the obvious. Do not talk about what you are going to do; do it. When you talk about what you intend to communicate, the energy goes into the talking and not into the doing. We are working in movement to learn how much we can convey without language. We move because we feel a particular emotion and often movement preceeds rational understanding. This is especially true in a movement class if we are sensitive to what is happening around us. This sensitivity is absolutely basic to sensory perception, fine acting and full living.

We sometimes think of non-verbal communication as giving appropriate messages but we must also be concerned with receiving sensitively so we can send messages selectively and purposefully. If an actor's movement pattern fails to communicate the desired emotion to his fellow actors, he might ask himself the following questions:

1. Are you observing the people around you to see how they act and react?
2. Are you observing yourself to determine tension

levels and responses in your own body?

3. Are you analyzing emotional situations to determine whether double level tension should be employed to communicate what you feel? (Double level tension occurs when there is a surface emotion or state covering up an inner emotion. For example, this would happen if you were afraid and did not want to show it.)

4. Are you giving proper emphasis to environmental influences? One behaves differently with familiar people and places than when they are not familiar.

5. Are you aware of psychological interrelationships and their effects on you? (An interrelationship is a reciprocal relationship like a father to a son, a woman to a man. When we talk about the psychological aspect we are talking about the intangibles of emotion, attitude, and connection. All relationships can be said to have psychological overtones but some are more important and affective than others.)

Although mind and body are one, a person has to believe he can do something before he will try it. If a new experience is to be tried, he must trust his teacher and the group with whom he is learning. Touching another person in human experience is always motivated by some emotional attitude or feeling. In fear we may reach out for support from a friend; in anger we may strike away an attacker. We have come to use certain kinds of touching to mean certain kinds of emotions. A kiss on the mouth indicates a special closeness; a kiss on the hand, merely etiquette. In acting class, a sense of honesty will dictate what is propitious and what is not. Touching which does not come out of conscious exploitation is what gives the actor freedom to explore communication through physical contact.

We are all sexual beings. Although most contact between man and woman is sexual in some circumstances, the sexual is only one of many responses. If the actor limits his physical contact to show only sexual feelings, he is cutting off a whole rich area of communication to his fellow actors and to his audience. Using physical contact he can show tenderness, concern, compassion, uncertainty, fear, anger, and much, much more. Therefore the actor must use the acting class and his fellow students to explore all kinds of physical contact without limiting himself to one kind of response. The following exercises are planned to provide experiences for the actor to explore without cliche, preconceived emotional involvement or predetermined response.

NON-VERBAL COMMUNICATION

Before the actor can communicate thoughts, attitudes, and emotions, he must know what factors influence movement communication. These factors are listed below so that the actor can use them to explore their effect on movement ideas.

Focus

Focus involves not only the use of the eyes, but can mean the main point of interest. For example: a person, sitting down, reaches behind him and touches something strange. He may not dare to turn to look. The audience will be watching his hand, not where he is looking. Therefore the focus is his hand. An actor can steal a whole scene by focusing improperly.

Direction

Direction involves the thrust of the action; up, down, around diagonally, forward, or backward.

Level

Levels are usually divided into three main parts; standing, sitting, and lying. These are also designated as high, middle, and low.

Dynamics

Dynamics involves the flow of action, the rhythm of what is going on. The actor should learn to be aware of what dynamics are needed and how to help create them.

Pace

Pace is a general term which applies to the overall tempo of a scene or an act. As such, it allows for variety in rhythms, just as an adagio movement (pace) in a sonata nevertheless can include accelerations and retards (rhythms).

Energy

The amount of energy used can change the interpretation of a movement. The same walk performed either tensely or with relaxation communicates two different ideas.

NON-VERBAL COMMUNICATION...CONTACT

Exercise 1—Physical Contact...Interdependency.

Purpose

To explore movement possibilities working with interdependency (self and partner.)

Exercise

Work with a partner in a way that you could not do by yourself. Both must support each other regardless of size or weight disparity. Try working in place as well as covering distance.

Suggestions

Some examples of this kind of movement might be: walking while leaning back to back, walking with three legs instead of four, or doing back bends holding each other's wrists. Both partners must be active all the time. Try this with three or more people. How does the addition of people change the activity? Make sure you explore all possibilities of support besides holding wrists. (Holding wrists instead of hands generally gives better support.) Try to think of situations that would require interdependency. Try working with people both bigger and smaller than yourself. What difference does it make in your feelings about what you are doing?

NON-VERBAL COMMUNICATION. . .CONTACT

Exercise 2—Physical Contact. . .Tangling

Purpose

To learn to cooperate while exploring non-verbal activities.

Exercise

Work with a partner. Assume a starting position that involves physical contact. Tangle yourselves as much as possible without letting go of each other. When you are as tangled as you can be, untangle without letting go. Also work without a definite starting position. See how much distance you can cover in the tangled position.

Suggestions

Try working with more than two people. Try working in place to see how many levels you can use while remaining tangled. See how much distance you can use. Try using different kinds of sounds. Try working with two groups of tangles. Can the two groups absorb each other with ease? What kinds of feeling do you have when you work with great tension, or as little as possible?

NON-VERBAL COMMUNICATION. . .CONTACT

Exercise 3—Physical Contact. . .Floating

Purpose
To explore mutual trust.

Exercise
Our backs are very strong. A 115 pound girl can carry a 200 pound man on her back if she knows how to do it. The bottom person should have the buttocks of the top person in the small of the back. Linking elbows for support, the bottom person bends over, bending the knees slightly, and carries the top person. The top person should relax, close his eyes and breathe quietly as the bottom person moves slowly up and down by bending and slightly straightening the knees. Do not lock the knees. Reverse positions letting the top person become the bottom person, etc.

Suggestions
This exercise is very good for stretching the back and relieving tensions. Work slowly and gently to avoid sudden stress. Start working with people who are close to your own size and gradually work with bigger people.

Establishing rapport, relaxing tension while working back over back

NON-VERBAL COMMUNICATION. . .CONTACT

Exercise 4—Physical Contact

Purpose

To begin to learn how to touch another person on stage without inhibition.

Exercise

This exercise is best done in a group. Close your eyes and keep them closed. Start out apart from everyone else. Move slowly, with your hands in front of you. When you contact someone, react vigorously in any manner you choose, so that an observer can tell that there has been physical contact. Keep touching and reacting with your eyes closed. To avoid working with the same people, turn to face a different direction.

Suggestions

If the action of the group gets too fast and furious, stop. Relax, separate and start again. The eyes should stay closed to enable you to concentrate on the sensory experience of touch. If the group has difficulty keeping a slow pace, try working to music that is slow and unaccented. People can use their voices as accompaniment to help keep the slow pace and to provide interesting variations.

NON-VERBAL COMMUNICATION. . .CONTACT

Exercise 5—Physical Contact

Purpose

To learn to use touch for physical information such as height, weight, age (young or old), sex.

Exercise

Repeat the experience of keeping your eyes closed and touching in a group. Instead of reacting vigorously when you touch continue touching. Use your hands to find out about the person you are touching. Is he old or young? Does he have flabby or firm hands? Is he fat or thin? Male or female? Is he dressed roughly or finely?

Suggestions

After you have answered, by touch, some of the questions asked, stop. Open your eyes, and see how accurate you were. If you missed a great deal try again. Avoid using any vocal sounds.

Exercise 6—Physical Contact

Purpose

To learn to touch someone with eyes open without inhibition.

Exercise

Repeat the experience of touching in a group, reacting vigorously to contact. This time keep your eyes open. Vary the way you touch, and the way you react to being touched. Use sounds to help add variety.

Suggestions

What happens when you open your eyes? Does it make you feel strange? Why? Work on this exercise until the touching becomes natural and easy.

NON-VERBAL COMMUNICATION. . .CONTACT

Exercise 7—Emotional Contact

Purpose
To learn how to establish contact without actually touching another person.

Exercise
Work with another person. Without talking, let one person establish himself as leader, the other, as follower. As the leader establishes a direction of movement, the other follows. The leader can also move with different degrees of tension which the partner should also follow. After working for a while change places so the follower becomes leader, and the leader becomes the follower.

Suggestions
It is not important to copy the exact movement. What is important is to be sensitive to the direction, tension, and scope of the movement established by the leader. In order really to get something out of this exercise both must concentrate totally on what they are doing.

NON-VERBAL COMMUNICATION. . .CONTACT

Exercise 8—Emotional Contact

Purpose

To learn to be sensitive to nuances in movement.

EXERCISE

Repeat Exercise 7 (p. 124). This time the leadership should shift back and forth without actually stopping and changing. For example: if one person establishes a direction of up, the other would go up, but when he decides to go in a different direction or with a different quality of tension, the other would then follow him. This is quite difficult to do and in the beginning may resemble a tug of war. Work without a story or emotion in mind. Concentrate on direction, level, and tension.

Suggestions

People watching this exercise should get the feeling that the two people working are very involved with each other. They may see an emotion or a story; this is perfectly valid. To avoid cliche, however, no story should be established before the actors start working. If actors have trouble shifting the leadership, they should go back to Exercise 4 and watch for cues that tell them what to do. Then start Exercise 5 again working slowly and with total concentration. With practice, it will work.

NON-VERBAL COMMUNICATION. . .CONCENTRATION

The rest of the exercises in non-verbal communication are all best done in a group to achieve maximum benefit. Up to now, the concentration has been on the individual or on the individual and a partner. When you add to this two-part concentration a third aspect it becomes quite difficult. In these exercises the actor will have to concentrate on what the entire group is doing. On stage, he cannot always look at what is going on, yet he must always be aware of what is happening. In these exercises, as on stage, the actor cannot always look at what is going on. But he must learn to feel what is happening and react appropriately.

These group exercises and improvisations all assume that the actors have warmed up together and are attuned to one another. Actors should be aware that clarity of purpose is essential. This is particularly a problem when working in larger groups. Clarity is achieved by focusing on the specific purpose of the exercise and by maintaining the concentration (individual—partner—group, or individual—group—leader). Let ideas from the group suggest other ways to practice concentration. Those included here are merely ideas to get started.

NON-VERBAL COMMUNICATION. . .CONCENTRATION

Exercise 9—Concentration on direction of movement.

Purpose
To learn to be sensitive to movement changes within a group.

Exercise
Work in groups of four to six people. Establish physical contact. Without talking, try to evolve a common direction of movement. As in Exercise 7, (p. 124) this direction can be changed but it should be done slowly to avoid the appearance of wrestling. No one should be appointed leader, whether verbally or by intimation. If one person constantly dominates the group, change the groups so that this cannot happen.

Suggestions
Directions can be up, down, forward, backward, circular, diagonal, or any other way. Do not let the direction be changed before it is fully and clearly established. Try this exercise without physical contact.

NON-VERBAL COMMUNICATION. . .CONCENTRATION

Exercise 10—Concentration on tension levels in movement.

Purpose

To learn to be sensitive to changes of tension level in movement within the group.

Exercise

Work in groups of four to six people. Establish physical contact. Without talking evolve a common tension level such as relaxation, great tension, or erratic tension. Once the tension level is clearly established, change it. Work slowly and avoid wrestling with each other unless this is the effect you want to create. Do not work with emotional words in mind such as hate, fear, or love.

Suggestions

An observer ought to be able to perceive clearly the tension changes. Avoid letting your faces indicate the tension change. What happens to the face should be the result of the total body change in tension level. Try this exercise without physical contact.

NON-VERBAL COMMUNICATION. . .CONCENTRATION

Exercise 11—Concentration on changes of sound within the group.

Purpose
To learn to be sensitive to sound changes within the group.

Exercise
Work in groups of four to six people. Establish physical contact. Without prior discussion, make sounds until a common sound evolves. Once this sound is clearly established, try to evolve another sound. Move with the sounds. Do not use words.

Suggestions
If more than one group is working at the same time, keep the sound level low enough so that each group can hear its own. It is fairly difficult to hear a sound and not use it but try not to be influenced by the sounds you hear from other groups. Try this without physical contact. Let the movement come from the quality of the sound. A hiss might suggest one kind of movement, grunts, another.

NON-VERBAL COMMUNICATION. . .CONCENTRATION

Exercise 12—Concentration on movement, tension level, and sound changes within the group.

Purpose

To learn to be sensitive to nuances of movement, tension level, and sound within the group.

Exercise

Start out as far apart from each other as you can be, using as many different levels as possible. Some people can be lying, others kneeling, others sitting or standing. Move toward the center of the room, When you get to the center, slowly start reaching up. When the group can reach no more, and the tension level is as high as possible, let all the tension go and completely relax. Do not push into the center, work with one another rather than as separate individuals. Try it again using the voice to augment the upward movement from the center.

Suggestions

You can use sound from the very beginning to accompany the movement. The sounds used will affect the quality of the movement. Try this exercise both with and without physical contact.

NON-VERBAL COMMUNICATION. . .RELATIONSHIPS

Actors begin to learn to communicate thoughts, attitudes, and feelings through the use of movement sequence. Movement sequence is a short pattern of movement comparable to a sentence in speech. It can be simple or complex depending upon the student's ability, but he must be able to repeat the sequence exactly the same way each time he does it. This enables the actor to use one or more of the factors discussed previously in order to vary what is being communicated. When speaking, it is possible to say "I love you," with several different inflections, each meaning something quite different. This is what the actor learns to do when he repeats his movement sequence, varying a different factor each time.

Once the actor feels comfortable about creating movement sequences, he should then try to use these movement sequences in relationship to others. How is his movement sequence affected by the sequence of another or others? By trying to evoke feelings in others without resorting to convention, the student finds unlimited ways to show his feelings or attitudes. The actor will learn to analyze emotions in movement terms. For example, fear produces high tension, the desire to protect one's body, a folding in on oneself. Anger also produces high tension, but the movements seemingly are outward, strong, and not entirely controlled. By experimenting in the classroom, the actors will learn what kinds of feeling can be conveyed through the use of great energy or little energy. They will discover which emotions produce outward movements and which require inward movement. This will make their stage work clearer, fresher, and more convincing.

NON-VERBAL COMMUNICATION. . .RELATIONSHIPS

Exercise 13—Communication of feelings through the use of movement.

Purpose

To learn to communicate feelings in movement and to remember movement through the use of the kinesthetic sense.

Exercise

Make up a movement sequence. Keep it very simple in the beginning. Work on it until you can repeat it exactly without being conscious of each tiny piece of movement. Keep repeating it until you begin to get an attitude about what you are doing. If this does not happen, arbitrarily work at high or low tension levels and see if this helps.

Suggestions

An observer ought to be able to see a difference in your movements between simply repeating the movement and repeating the movements after you have developed an attitude about what you are doing. It is not important that the observer be able to say, ''you are happy,'' or '' you are sad.'' It is enough that he see your involvement.

Exercise 14—Communication of feelings through the use of movement.

Purpose

To learn to communicate feelings through movement and to be sensitive to the way the movement of others affects one.

Exercise

Pick a partner and work back to back or in such a way that neither of you can see what the other is doing. Independently work out a movement sequence. Face each other and repeat your own movement sequence with the feelings you had worked out on your own. Do not change the movements but if you feel different emotionally, you may change the tension level, focus, or dynamics as is felt necessary to respond to the stimulus of your partner.

Suggestions

How did the other person's movement affect you? If it did not, why not? Experiment with the factors affecting movement if you are having trouble evoking feelings in yourself during the time you are doing the movement sequence.

Exercise 15—Communication of feelings through the use of movement.

Purpose

To learn to communicate feelings through movement and to be aware of the factors that influence movement communication.

Exercise

Repeat Exercise 13 (p. 132) but make up a new movement sequence. Work both with and without physical contact. Add the use of the voice as you choose. Experiment with changing levels, direction, or pace. No matter what factors you choose to work with, do not change the basic movement sequence. Keep it clear always or the movements will become obscure.

Suggestions

Observers watching the interaction of partners should get a real sense of involvement. If this does not happen you should start over. Do the movement sequence, add the inflection (feelings that come from the movement), then work with your partner. The more complex the movement sequence, the more possibility of real interaction. Do not make your movement sequence so complicated that you cannot repeat it exactly the same way each time.

NON-VERBAL COMMUNICATION. . .RELATIONSHIPS

Exercise 16—Double level tension.

Purpose
To explore and learn to recognize double level tension.

Exercise
Double level tension exists when there is an inner tension that is sublimated to an outer tension. In THE CRUCIBLE, Elizabeth loves John Procter but does not know how to express it. She seems somewhat hard and cold, but her love has to come through in places, or her character will be one-dimensional. Establish an inner tension. Sublimate this inner tension so that you can project a different level of tension.

Suggestions
This exercise is extremely difficult. You are accomplishing a great deal if you can begin to recognize double level tension in others. Double level tension is used, onstage, to achieve emotional nuance.

NON-VERBAL COMMUNICATION. . .RELATIONSHIPS

Exercise 17—Use of dynamics in working as a group.

Purpose
To explore the use of dynamics in group improvisation.

Exercise
Separate around the room so that everyone has room to move. Work so that everyone tries to use a different level. At different tempos, move toward the center of the room using your body in as many kinds of movements as you can. When you reach the center, build tension and let your body rise as high as you can. When the peak of your movement is reached, swirl down to the floor in a partial or total collapse. Work individually so that everyone does not collapse at the same time. Try this both with and without sounds. Work both with and without physical contact.

Suggestions
Try repeating this exercise without stopping. This is accomplished by having the people collapse, then work out toward the periphery of the room. When everyone is out of the center, without stopping the feeling of motion, start again. This exercise can be done either with or without a leader.

NON-VERBAL COMMUNICATION. . .RELATIONSHIPS

Exercise 18—Use of tempo in working as a group.

Purpose
To explore the use of tempo in group improvisation

Exercise
Establish a beat, as a group, that is quite lively. Maintain the beat as you do various movements like bounces, strikes, or swirls. See how much rhythmic variation you can achieve within the pace. Work closely together, both with and without physical contact. Work both with and without vocal sounds. Use different physical levels. The main point is to see how much variety of movement you can achieve within a given tempo. Not all the movements have to be fast even if the underlying pulse is fast.

Suggestions
It is difficult to move and maintain a beat at the same time. See what you need to do in order to keep the pulse audible. It is even more difficult if you work without visual contact.

NON-VERBAL COMMUNICATION. . .RELATIONSHIPS

Exercise 19—Use of meter in working as a group.

Purpose
To explore the interrelationship of different rhythmic patterns within one general pattern.

Exercise
Use a meter, such as 4/4. Let one person move as the whole note (4 counts per movement), the next person move as the half-note (2 counts per movement), the next person move as the quarter-note (one count per movement), the next person move as the eighth-note (two movements per count). Move in a circle so that after four measures (sixteen counts) each person is back in his starting position. This is called a canon. It should be practiced until everyone is comfortable doing each note value. If you wish you may add sixteenth-notes, moving four times for each count. You can change the meter to 5/4, 3/4, 7/8, etc. In each case, the second part of the meter indicates which note has one move. In 5/4 it is the quarter-note with five counts per measure. In 7/8 it is the eighth-note with seven counts per measure.

Suggestions
After everyone feels comfortable with the whole idea, try moving the note value in a particular way rather than just walking or running.

NON-VERBAL COMMUMICATION. . .RELATIONSHIPS

Exercise 20—Using a canon to explore interrelationship.

Purpose

To demonstrate how many different rhythmic patterns can be developed within one given meter.

Exercise

Use a meter, such as 4/4. Each member of the group should develop a rhythmic pattern by himself that can fit the given meter. First clap the pattern until it can be repeated with ease. Then develop a movement pattern that can be repeated using the whole body and the voice. When each member of the group has his pattern, fit them all together so that there is either physical or emotional contact among all the members of the group. Repeat the action until some kind of attitude develops. Try moving the group, using different levels, direction, and focus. Each member of the group must maintain his own rhythm with clarity, so that there is a sense of all the parts fitting together to make a whole. This exercise demonstrates how each character in a play, with his own rhythm or beat, fits into the general framework. The director must help each character to be distinct, yet remain a part of the ensemble.

NON-VERBAL COMMUNICATION. . .RELATIONSHIPS

Exercise 21—Working with props.

Purpose

To find extraordinary uses for ordinary objects.

Exercise

Work with a chair and explore the possible ways you can use it without using it to sit on. Develop a movement sequence. Repeat the sequence until an attitude or emotion evolves. Place another person with a chair near you. Do your sequences with emotional contact. Experiment and put the chairs in varying positions. How does this affect what you do and feel? Repeat the exercise using many students working at the same time. Work with and without sounds. Use different levels to achieve more interesting designs.

Suggestions

Other props that might be used are:
1. long pieces of heavy material.
2. elastic tape at least ten yards or longer.
3. anything already in or part of the room in which you are working.
4. sticks or boards.
5. big cartons, such as those from refrigerators.
6. common children's toys, such as hoops, big balls, or toy instruments.
7. assortment of common objects in everyday use.
8. rehearsal props.

Use the props to stimulate non-verbal improvisations. Try to achieve a variety of situations using sounds both as accompaniment and communication.

NON-VERBAL COMMUNICATION. . .RELATIONSHIPS

Exercise 22—Environmental influences.

Purpose

To explore the effect environment has on behavior.

Exercise

We are all affected by our environment to some extent. Environmental influences include weather, location, or the behavior of people around us. Actors should become aware of how they react to environmental changes. Are you affected by movies or books or theatre to the extent that you feel like one of the characters? Establish an environment such as a haunted house, a park, a mental hospital, or a place of your choosing. Talk only to establish the general environment. Do not describe it in words or assign roles. Let the actors involved communicate the kind of hospital, park, etc. by their behavior, their relationships to one another, and their physical movements.

Suggestions

The environment and its effect on the behavior of those in it should be explored without words. Those in the class who watch ought to be able to recognize the reactions of the participants. Work with total concentration. Try evolving a non-verbal improvisation with a definite end. Although very difficult to work out without prior discussion, this will help the actors to be more sensitive to one another. Try creating physical environments, such as walking on hot pavement, walking on ice, climbing rocks, etc. Also think about empty rooms, crowded buses, waiting rooms, or stalled elevators.

NON-VERBAL COMMUNICATION. . .RELATIONSHIPS

Exercise 23—Psychological interrelationships.

Purpose

To become aware of psychological interrelationships and their effect on others.

Exercise

An interrelationship is a reciprocal relationship. This means all concerned are actively involved in giving and receiving. In a psychological interrelationship we deal with emotions and intangibles. We can often learn more about a complex relationship by watching and feeling movement than by listening to words which may or may not be accurate. Establish an interrelationship with another person without words. This is done by one person establishing a mood, action, or response which is then picked up by the partner. Try to carry the relationship to some kind of ending even if it is not a solution.

Try this again using a real or imaginary third person coming into the established activity or a new activity. What happens to the relationship between the first two? How is the third person affected by the other two?

Suggestions

This exercise requires much concentration. Do not talk about any part of it until the exercise is completed. If you focus on your partner or partners you will be able to invent a situation without talking about it ahead of time. Those watching ought to be able to recognize the emotional contact established.

NON-VERBAL COMMUNICATION. . .RELATIONSHIPS

Exercise 24—Creating non-verbal improvisations from physical positions.

Purpose

To learn to create improvisations with imagination without predetermined attitudes.

Exercise

Each person, running as fast as possible toward a wall, should freeze before he hits it. When everyone has enough control, do this work in groups of three to five. This time, when each person freezes he should establish physical or emotional contact with the others in the groups. Remember the positions and go somewhere in the room to work. Establish a non-verbal improvisation using the starting positions and relationships to suggest a direction.

Suggestions

Use sounds where appropriate to help establish an environment. Repeat the exercise with different people and positions.

NON-VERBAL COMMUNICATION. . .RELATIONSHIPS

Exercise 25—Assuming a mask.

Purpose
To learn how to create and use a facial mask in preparation for working with a real mask.

Exercise
Working in front of a mirror, experiment with a variety of faces until you find one which interests you. Practice assuming the mask with your eyes away from the mirror, then check your accuracy. When you are sure you can control your face, work to find an appropriate body. Practice how this new person would walk, sit, climb stairs, get past a mud puddle, etc.

Suggestions
Work silently until you are sure you can use sound without losing your face. At first your face will tire quickly. Stop frequently and relax your facial muscles until they grow strong enough to work as long as you wish.

NON-VERBAL COMMUNICATION. . .RELATIONSHIPS

Exercise 26—Using a mask.

Purpose

To learn to use a mask in preparation for working with a real mask.

Exercise

Procede as in Exercise 25 (p. 144). Create an objective for your character. Practice it until you feel comfortable with your character. Work with a partner whose objective conflicts with yours. Explore how your character might solve this problem. Find an alternative, preferably opposite, approach for the same character. Try working with more than one other person. What difficulties does this present? Try working with other characters. How does this affect your work?

Suggestions

These exercises alone will not prepare a student to work with a mask, but will help strengthen facial muscles and give him a sense of what it is like to work with a mask. Experiment with a variety of faces and try to remember what is done to avoid getting into a rut.

NON-VERBAL COMMUNICATION. . .RELATIONSHIPS

Exercise 27—Making machines.

Purpose
To learn to work imaginatively with a group; to be aware of spatial relationships.

Exercise
Create a machine like a toaster, typewriter, or any other that comes to mind. Make sure you physicalize the distinctive action. What makes it a toaster and not a mixer? After the initial machine is decided upon do not talk about who will be what part. This is hard to do so work slowly and resist the temptation to verbalize although sounds that are appropriate should be used.

Suggestions
Make machines that are imaginary. Try having them produce a product. Try starting your machines by having someone making a sound and a movement. Each person will, in turn, connect himself by sound and movement. Try breaking down. Explore all kinds of possibilities other than total collapse.

146

NON-VERBAL COMMUNICATION. . .RELATIONSHIPS

Exercise 28—"Playing age."

Purpose

To learn what kind of specifics must be considered in order to play someone whose age is different from your own.

Exercise

Set an action for yourself. Play it as you normally would. Now pick someone whose age is not your own. What kinds of information do you need to have in order to play this new age validly? What makes an old person old? Is there a difference between a twenty year-old and a thirty-five year-old that is true for every twenty and thirty-five year-old? Before one can "play age," one has to know the answers to these questions.

Suggestions

This impossible exercise is common to acting classes. Actors usually resort to cliche because they try to play a generalized concept that has no real validity. The same attention to detail to play objectives is also necessary to play different ages. "Playing age" as such is impossible.

CHAPTER FIVE

USE OF EXERCISE IN REHEARSAL AND PERFORMANCE

Many students find it difficult to come to rehearsals and performances without bringing all their worries with them. It is a real problem for them to achieve the proper energy level required by their role without wasting rehearsal time. A common criticism of productions is that the actors loosened up and performed well only after the opening scenes of the play. No actor should use the first few minutes of a play to get ready to work. This should all be done ahead of time with the whole cast. All artists prepare themselves before they work: dancers warm up, musicians warm themselves and their instruments, artists arrange their tools so that they may work without interruption. Like artists, actors, too, must prepare.

Movement warmups by the whole cast, performed together, can help solve the problem of preparation. The actor who uses movement effectively can change depression into the greatest joy if this is what is needed. How? Analyze the kind of movement found in depression; slow, close to the body, seemingly unmotivated. Being joyful requires activity, quick, sprightly movements full of energy and vitality. To make the transition from depression to joy, try doing some jumps, bounces, or leaps for as long as necessary. It might take fifteen minutes. Work with others in the cast who need to be joyful or energetic. Use your whole body: your arms, head, torso, and legs. You will find that the change in movement, if you concentrate on what you are doing, will transform your mood. By using movement as a group, before the rehearsal or performance, contact is made in the most basic sense, with one's fellow actors. The group becomes one, each in tune with the others, and with what is happening. They are able to share in the process of creating the magic implicit in performance.

Using movement exercise as a pre-textual conditioning also helps increase stamina, develops proper tension levels, and enables the director to establish unity. As a group you can do warmups or any of the exercises previously described. The following exercises have proven to work particularly well as pre-rehearsal activities. Set the pace according to the mood required by the play. Whatever activities you choose, concentrate on yourself, your partner and the group. Through this rapport, you and your fellow players will begin the performance or rehearsal with a common feeling about what you wish to communicate.

REHEARSAL AND PERFORMANCE EXERCISES

Exercise 1—Using non-verbal communication.

Purpose
To use the eyes and body to communicate.

Exercise
Sit anywhere in the room making sure that you are able to see everyone. Without talking, use your eyes to contact a partner. When you have your partner, get together and begin to warm up using any exercise you wish. Do not discuss which exercise you plan to use, just do it. If both people start on a different exercise, non-verbally agree which one you will do. Keep changing exercises as you feel you want to, but always work non-verbally. This does not preclude sounds, only words.

Suggestions
Try changing partners after each exercise. Do not use words to indicate that an exercise is finished. Try not to use mime or mouth words to indicate a new activity. You can indicate you are ready to change partners by staying quiet when you and your partner are finished. Work out other variations but avoid using stock gestures such as shrugging shoulders.

REHEARSAL AND PERFORMANCE EXERCISES

Exercise 2—Shoulder stand.

Purpose
To increase circulation and relieve fatigue.

Exercise
Lie on the floor on your back. Keeping back on floor, lift legs to right angle with torso. Using arms for support, lift lower back and buttocks off the floor, pointing toes to the ceiling. Try to keep the back as straight as possible. To relieve unnecessary neck tension talk to yourself, which will also help to keep your breathing steady. Try to stay in this position for at least three minutes.

Suggestions
This is an exercise used in Yoga. It helps to focus on the present, letting the troubles and tensions of the earlier part of the day recede. Keeping the basic position try working without the support of your arms and hands. Work with a partner in this position, and see what kind of movement you can evolve.

REHEARSAL AND PERFORMANCE EXERCISES

Exercise 3—Headstand.

Purpose
To increase circulation and relieve fatigue.

Exercise
Sit on your knees. Place your head down in front of you as close to your knees as possible. Clasp your hands on the floor on top of your head and walk your feet up until your hips are aligned with your head in a straight line. Bend your knees to your chest and slowly extend the knees until your legs are fully extended above the head. To come down, reverse the procedure working slowly and in control.

Suggestions
This is a very difficult exercise. Work with control. If you should find yourself falling, tuck your head and do a forward roll. This exercise can be done on any type of floor but for beginners a mat or flat cushion is recommended. When you can do the exercise with bent knees, try working with the legs straight. This is much more difficult and requires strong torso muscles.

REHEARSAL AND PERFORMANCE EXERCISES

Exercise 4—Free falls.

Purpose
To increase self-confidence, establish group rapport.

Exercise
Have one person stand on a desk or table that is steady. The rest of the group (at least eight or ten, depending on the person's weight and the height of the fall) should stand in two lines facing each other, arms extended, in front of the jumper. The person should fall and be caught by the group. The person who is jumping should have his arms by his side or extended in front of his face. Let each person try jumping sideways, backward, and forward. Vary the heights and time of catching. The longer the group waits to catch the jumper, the more frightening it is. When the group and jumpers are proficient, let the jumper dive into the group. Naturally this should not be attempted until everyone is ready.

Suggestions
If a person is really afraid, respect and understand this. Work carefully and slowly until the fear is allayed. The catchers should not hold their arms rigid but allow their whole bodies to give a bit to absorb the impact of the falling body. For extra support, catchers can hold one anothers' wrists.

REHEARSAL AND PERFORMANCE EXERCISES

Exercise 5—Circle swaying.

Purpose

Increase self-confidence, establish group rapport, strengthen kinesthetic sense.

Exercise

One person should stand in the center of a circle that is formed by everyone sitting with his legs extended to the standing person. The sitters should press their feet against the legs of the person standing. The standing person should cross his arms in front of his chest and let himself be passed around the circle by the sitters. The standing person should keep the torso lifted. If it begins to bend either forward or backward, the group should point this out so that it can be corrected. Each member of the group should have a turn being passed around.

Suggestions

If the person being passed around is very heavy, some members of the group can get behind the sitters to reinforce them. Work slowly and carefully especially in the beginning, or if someone is afraid. Work with eyes open as well as closed.

Establishing confidence through a free fall

REHEARSAL AND PERFORMANCE EXERCISES

Exercise 6—Group changes directed by internal signals.

Purpose
To establish group rapport.

Exercise
Run as fast as you can in one direction, but stop before you touch the wall. Try this as a group but start slowly in order to establish placement. Work up speed so that you start and stop as a group without sloppiness. Try this again but at a prearranged time or place, changing level or direction or both. Use sound to highlight changes. At no time should it appear that one person is leading the group.

Suggestions
This exercise is very useful when the group is working on crowd scenes. Each member of the group must concentrate on the others for maximum effect.

REHEARSAL AND PERFORMANCE EXERCISES

Exercise 7— Group improvisations directed by internal signals.

Purpose
To learn how to use group rapport.

Exercise
Repeat Exercise 6 (p. 157), but this time let two groups work at the same time. Create a non-verbal improvisation as a group. Try to avoid one person's dominance. Experiment with both physical and emotional contact. Do not force a particular situation.

Suggestions
If the group improvisations always turn into something literal, such as a fight or a tug-of-war, work to music or concentrate on the way a particular movement feels. Use the concepts of level, focus, direction, dynamics, etc., to help you.

REHEARSAL AND PERFORMANCE EXERCISES

Exercise 8—Group bounce.

Purpose
To relieve personal and group tension and fatigue.

Exercise
Start by lying on the floor. Slowly begin to bounce one part of the body at a time until the whole body is bouncing. Gradually, keeping the bounce as much as possible, stand up. Continue bouncing until you come in contact with another person. Mutually adjust your bouncing to each other. Gradually, two should become four and continue until the whole group is bouncing together. Use sound as accompaniment.

Suggestions
Many of the warmups such as stretching, collapsing, etc. can be done as a group activity to relieve tension and fatigue. This one seems particularly good because it generally makes people laugh.

REHEARSAL AND PERFORMANCE EXERCISES

Exercise 9—Free association with words and movement.

Purpose

To relax members of the group, to encourage good vocal articulation while moving, to stimulate imagination.

Exercise

Use the diagonal of the room to make the longest working space. One at a time members of the group should go across the room speaking one word clearly while doing a movement pattern. Both the word and the movement pattern should be repeated as the space permits. There should be no attempt to connect the word with the movement.

Suggestions

Students should experiment with vocal variety. The movement patterns should be varied as to tempo, size, tension level, and dynamics. Students watching should see if there is any connection between word and movement. Sometimes the word will sound like the movement rather than interpret it. All kinds of extremes of sounds and movement should be explored.

REHEARSAL AND PERFORMANCE EXERCISES

Exercise 10—Using free association with words and movement.

Purpose
To stimulate imagination, to increase group rapport.

Exercise
Repeat the previous exercise. Work with a partner. Each person should keep the same word and movement, but the dynamics and tension levels will probably change. Try many different partners exploring the effect these new partners have on your action, and feelings.

Suggestions
This exercise usually creates many funny situations. Should this occur you might want to try working very seriously with a straight face just to see how this affects your work. Try working with more than one partner to see how this changes your responses.

REHEARSAL AND PERFORMANCE EXERCISES

Exercises 11—Paper Bag Masks.

(Courtesy of Dorothy Sherman, Department of Dramatic Arts, University of Delaware.)

Purpose

To prepare actors to work with masks, to increase use of body, to communicate attitudes and feelings.

Exercise

Cut holes to fit each person's eyes and mouth. It is helpful to tie elastic around the neck of the bag to keep it on the head. Create non-verbal improvisations while wearing the paper bag. Note the effect of focus, direction, dynamics, and tension levels while working. Use sound to increase intensity.

Suggestions

It is very hard to sense what others in your group are doing while wearing a paper bag, because your peripheral vision is so limited. Learn how to use your head more effectively instead of relying on the corner of the eye. Paper bags cover all facial gesture which makes it hard to distinguish people. If you want to be easily recognized, experiment with body actions which achieve this. Try conveying a sense of age, compassion, anger, or horror. Avoid stock gesture. Create an action credible for your character.

REHEARSAL AND PERFORMANCE EXERCISES

Exercise 12—Follow the leader.

Purpose
To increase group rapport, stimulate imagination, and provide variety in physical warmup.

Exercise
Arrange the group in a circle or any formation that allows everyone to see one another. One person should begin an activity which the group should copy exactly. As soon as the group is doing this, someone in the group should initiate a new activity. Each new action should be offered spontaneously with no verbal designation as to which person should act as leader. Vary the actions as much as possible so that the whole body gets a warmup by the time the exercise is finished.

Suggestions
If the group has difficulty in settling on one action, work in slow motion. This exercise helps develop peripheral vision, which is necessary for good ensemble work. Some actors like to be the center of attention and will find this exercise difficult. The group should recognize this and help the actor relate better to the group.

REHEARSAL AND PERFORMANCE EXERCISES

Exercise 13—Group sounds.

Purpose
To relax group, establish rapport among group, explore sound possibilities.

Exercise
The group should be in a small clump but loose enough to work comfortably. The group should start making sounds that do not strain the voice such as whispers, clucking with the tongue, or other sounds that can be made with the cheeks, tongue, or lips. Gradually increase the volume of the sound until full volume without straining is reached. Experiment with sounds increasing and decreasing in intensity. Let the body move as you feel. Keep the movement confined to a small amount of space.

Suggestions
Do not strain your voice. Work for variety rather than volume.

164

REHEARSAL AND PERFORMANCE EXERCISES

Exercise 14—Group improvisation.

Purpose

To learn to react spontaneously as a group without losing focus.

Exercise

Divide into small groups of three to six depending on the size of the total group. Create non-verbal improvisations as a group which have a definite beginning and end. The group should be able to repeat the improvisation without great variation. Each group should share their improvisation with the rest of the actors. Those watching should respond in some way, by using sound to create a new environment, by acting as props or obstacles, etc. Those creating the improvisation must use the new situations by incorporating them into their work without losing their main purpose. The idea is not to destroy the improvisation but to help members of the group react flexibly and spontaneously without losing their connection to one another.

Suggestions

Keep the reactions to the improvisation clear, specific, and focused. The reactions do not have to be big or prolonged. Try to work without verbal cues.

REHEARSAL AND PERFORMANCE EXERCISES

Exercise 15—Using food as stimulation.

Purpose

To use the taste, texture, and sensation of eating or preparing food to find new ways of creating characterization.

Exercise

While eating or preparing food notice the texture. Try to translate the texture into a movement that can be repeated. Try doing the same thing with taste. How does a lemon make you feel like moving? How does the sensation of eating peanut butter make you want to move? Work out several movement patterns based on how various foods affect you. Try doing your movement pattern with another actor. How does his work affect yours? Try to translate the movement pattern into a real situation. For example: two actors who used peeling shrimp and eating honey became a mental patient and attendant. The original food stimulation became the take-off point for an involved improvisation.

Suggestions

Don't force yourself to find real-life equivalents, let them come from the movement pattern if you feel them. Try working from the character to find images in food to suggest ways of moving. Have actors bring in various kinds of food and let people taste them blindfolded. Have people react before finding out what it is they ate. Even if it is obvious, tasting without being able to see adds a dimension to the experience.

AFTERWORD

Like all books, this one must end. Its subject, however, must continue to be explored. The actor cannot bank physical competence; he must use his body continually, or it will become flabby, weak, and dull, a blunt and useless instrument. Even when the actor has mastered the techniques outlined here, and can maintain them, there are still new challenges to explore and new ideas to try. One must keep moving in order to stay front.

If the actor works with a sense of joy and openness, reacting spontaneously and honestly, then the privacy of class work and rehearsal will foster new possibilities for the public performance. The exercises in this book are meant to stimulate, not to define the actor's work. If an idea is good, it should serve as the springboard for better ideas. If these activities lead the actor to find new theatre techniques, THEATRE MOVEMENT: THE ACTOR AND HIS SPACE has accomplished its purpose.

INDEX OF EXERCISES

The author working with her students